# Collins
# BELFAST

## Contents

Published by Collins
An imprint of HarperCollins Publishers
Westerhill Road, Bishopbriggs, Glasgow G64 2QT

www.harpercollins.co.uk

Copyright © HarperCollins Publishers Ltd 2020

Revised Edition 2020

Collins® is a registered trademark of HarperCollins Publishers Limited

Mapping generated from Collins Bartholomew digital databases

This Intellectual Property is based upon Crown Copyright and is reproduced
with the permission of Land & Property Services under Delegated Authority
from the Controller of Her Majesty's Stationery Office, © Crown Copyright
and database right (2019) Permit No.170072.

Belfast population derived from Population Estimates for UK, Mid-2018.
Source: Office for National Statistics licensed under the
Open Government Licence.

Fixed speed camera information supplied by PocketGPSWorld.Com Ltd

The contents of this publication are believed correct at the time of printing.
Nevertheless, the publisher can accept no responsibility for errors or
omissions, changes in the detail given, or for any expense or loss thereby
caused.

HarperCollins does not warrant that any website mentioned in this title will
be provided uninterrupted, that any website will be error free, that defects will
be corrected, or that the website or the server that makes it available are free
of viruses or bugs. For full terms and conditions please refer to the site terms
provided on the website.

The representation of a road, track or footpath is no evidence of a right of way.

Printed in China

ISBN 978 0 00 836999 6      Imp 001

e-mail: roadcheck@harpercollins.co.uk

Follow us @collins_ref

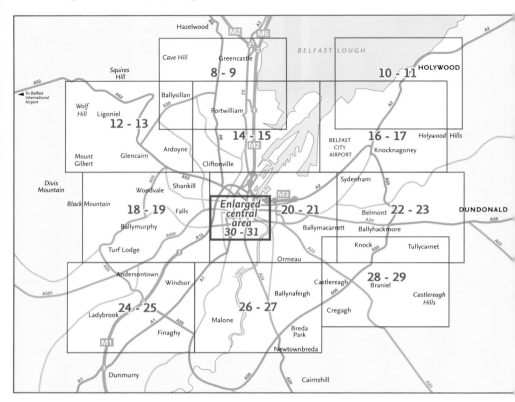

## Distance chart

The distance between two selected towns will be found at the intersection of the respective rows and columns, e.g distance between Belfast and Dublin is 104 miles/166 kilometres. In general, distances are based on the shortest routes by classified roads.

**DISTANCE IN KILOMETRES**

| | | | | | | | | | | | | | | | | | |
|---|---|---|---|---|---|---|---|---|---|---|---|---|---|---|---|---|---|
| 266 | 130 | 214 | 182 | 125 | 144 | 93 | 125 | 230 | 261 | 120 | 208 | 64 | 208 | 117 | 187 | 173 | Athlone |
| | 291 | 422 | 179 | 166 | 83 | 304 | 283 | 434 | 35 | 322 | 117 | 267 | 328 | 205 | 426 | 331 | Belfast |
| | | 283 | 150 | 242 | 251 | 80 | 248 | 293 | 326 | 182 | 221 | 189 | 349 | 86 | 285 | 296 | Castlebar |
| 141 | | | 400 | 256 | 323 | 208 | 147 | 86 | 459 | 104 | 426 | 152 | 206 | 334 | 118 | 125 | Cork |
| 81 | 182 | | | 221 | 157 | 203 | 307 | 405 | 189 | 294 | 69 | 245 | 389 | 66 | 408 | 355 | Donegal |
| 134 | 264 | 177 | | | 85 | 218 | 117 | 307 | 202 | 197 | 235 | 123 | 162 | 216 | 301 | 157 | Dublin |
| 114 | 112 | 94 | 250 | | | 237 | 197 | 350 | 118 | 240 | 155 | 186 | 245 | 166 | 344 | 242 | Dundalk |
| 78 | 104 | 151 | 160 | 138 | | | 155 | 192 | 339 | 104 | 270 | 109 | 272 | 138 | 162 | 219 | Galway |
| 90 | 52 | 157 | 202 | 98 | 53 | | | 197 | 318 | 112 | 333 | 50 | 99 | 243 | 213 | 48 | Kilkenny |
| 58 | 190 | 50 | 130 | 127 | 136 | 148 | | | 469 | 110 | 438 | 182 | 274 | 341 | 32 | 192 | Killarney |
| 78 | 177 | 155 | 92 | 192 | 72 | 123 | 97 | | | 358 | 115 | 301 | 363 | 240 | 462 | 366 | Larne |
| 144 | 271 | 183 | 54 | 253 | 192 | 219 | 120 | 123 | | | 346 | 74 | 210 | 230 | 104 | 128 | Limerick |
| 163 | 22 | 204 | 287 | 118 | 126 | 74 | 212 | 199 | 293 | | | 290 | 395 | 134 | 430 | 381 | Londonderry (Derry) |
| 75 | 201 | 114 | 65 | 184 | 123 | 150 | 65 | 70 | 69 | 224 | | | 160 | 181 | 176 | 109 | Roscrea |
| 130 | 73 | 138 | 266 | 43 | 147 | 97 | 169 | 208 | 274 | 72 | 216 | | | 325 | 290 | 82 | Rosslare |
| 40 | 167 | 118 | 95 | 153 | 77 | 116 | 68 | 31 | 114 | 188 | 46 | 181 | | | 285 | 291 | Sligo |
| 130 | 205 | 218 | 129 | 243 | 101 | 153 | 170 | 62 | 171 | 227 | 131 | 247 | 100 | | | 208 | Tralee |
| 73 | 128 | 54 | 209 | 41 | 135 | 104 | 86 | 152 | 213 | 150 | 144 | 84 | 113 | 203 | | | Waterford |
| 117 | 266 | 178 | 74 | 255 | 188 | 215 | 101 | 133 | 20 | 289 | 65 | 269 | 110 | 181 | 178 | | |
| 108 | 207 | 185 | 78 | 222 | 98 | 151 | 137 | 30 | 120 | 229 | 80 | 238 | 68 | 51 | 182 | 130 | |

**DISTANCE IN MILES**

# Key to map symbols 3

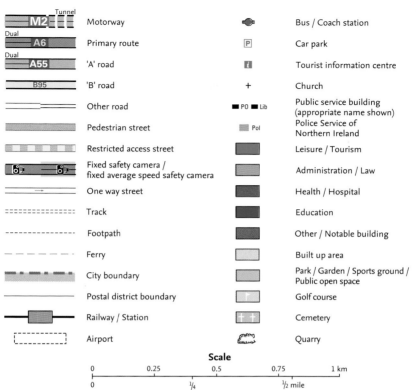

|  |  |  |  |
|---|---|---|---|
| M2 Tunnel | Motorway | (bus) | Bus / Coach station |
| Dual A6 | Primary route | P | Car park |
| Dual A55 | 'A' road | i | Tourist information centre |
| B95 | 'B' road | + | Church |
| | Other road | ■ PO ■ Lib | Public service building (appropriate name shown) |
| | Pedestrian street | Pol | Police Service of Northern Ireland |
| | Restricted access street | | Leisure / Tourism |
| camera | Fixed safety camera / fixed average speed safety camera | | Administration / Law |
| | One way street | | Health / Hospital |
| | Track | | Education |
| | Footpath | | Other / Notable building |
| | Ferry | | Built up area |
| | City boundary | | Park / Garden / Sports ground / Public open space |
| | Postal district boundary | | Golf course |
| | Railway / Station | † † | Cemetery |
| | Airport | | Quarry |

## Scale

0    0.25    0.5    0.75    1 km

0    ¼    ½ mile

**1:14,900   4¼ inches (10.8 cm) to 1 mile / 6.7 cm to 1 km**

## Key to map symbols (pages 4-5)

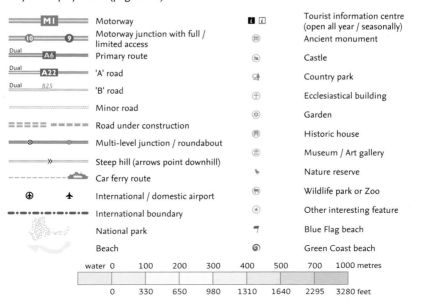

|  |  |  |  |
|---|---|---|---|
| M1 | Motorway | i i | Tourist information centre (open all year / seasonally) |
| 10 9 | Motorway junction with full / limited access | m | Ancient monument |
| Dual A6 | Primary route | (castle) | Castle |
| Dual A22 | 'A' road | (country park) | Country park |
| Dual B25 | 'B' road | ⊕ | Ecclesiastical building |
| | Minor road | ⊗ | Garden |
| | Road under construction | (historic house) | Historic house |
| ⊗ ○ | Multi-level junction / roundabout | (museum) | Museum / Art gallery |
| >> | Steep hill (arrows point downhill) | ↟ | Nature reserve |
| | Car ferry route | (zoo) | Wildlife park or Zoo |
| ⊕ ✈ | International / domestic airport | ⊛ | Other interesting feature |
| | International boundary | ⏋ | Blue Flag beach |
| | National park | ◉ | Green Coast beach |
| | Beach | | |

water 0    100    200    300    400    500    700    1000 metres

0    330    650    980    1310    1640    2295    3280 feet

ysteel · ROE VALLEY · Aghadowey · Finvoy · Dunloy · Newto · Cromm · Cloughmills
Lackagh · Glenhead · Drumsurn · Moneydig · Vow
Glenhead · B190 · B70 · B188 B207 · B70 · Clough
Gortnahey · Garvagh · B64 · Glarryford · M
Cross Roads · Craigavole · Bovedy · Kilrea · Craigs
Foreglen · Dungiven · Benbradagh 468 · B62 · B96 · M2
A6 · Boviel · Lislea · Cullybackey · Portglenone
laudy · BANAGHER GLEN · Swatragh · Tamlaght O'Crilly · Gracehill · B
Craigdarragh · B74 · A29 · Upperlands · Inishrush · A42 · Clady · Ahoghill · Cro
Feeny · Park · Mullaghmore 556 · Culnady · A42 · New Ferry · Straid
Maghera · Gulladuff · Lough Beg · Caddy
aght · Sawel Mt. 683 · Moneyneany · Knockcloghrim · R182 · Grange Corner · Moneyglass
ghcloga · Sperrin Mountains · B47 · Tobermore · A6 · Bellaghy · R182 · Roxhill · A26
Mount Hamilton · Draperstown · Curran · Castledawson · Toome · Randalstown
HERITAGE CENTRE · Cranagh · The Six Towns · Desertmartin · B40 · M22
Rousky · Glenhull · Slieve Gallion 528 · A31 · Magherafelt · Staffordstown · ANTRIM
Greencastle · Moneymore · The Loup · B18 · Ballyronan · A
Dunnamore · WELLBROOK BEETLING MILL · SPRINGHILL & COSTUME MUSEUM (NT) · BELFAST INTERNATIONAL · Aldergrove
Creggan · A505 · Lissan · Oritor · A29 · Derrychrin · Moortown · Crumli
N CREAGAN TOR CENTRE · Cookstown · Coagh · Ardboe · Glena
hmacrory · Carrickmore · Sandholes · Tullyhogue · The Diamond
nnakilly · Pomeroy · The Rock · B160 · Lough Neagh
Sixmilecross · Newmills · Stewartstown · Killeen · Mountjoy · Lower Ballinderry
Cappagh · Carland · Coalisland · OXFORD ISLAND · Aghalee
Mullaghmassa · Donaghmore · IRISH WORLD · Clonoe · Aughamullan · DISCOVERY CEN. · Aghagall
Slievemore 313 · Castlecaulfield · Ballynakilly · Maghery · Bannfoot · Soldierstow
ymackilroy · Dungannon · Granville · A45 · Milltown · Derrytrasna · Derrymacash
Ballygawley · Moygashel · Laghy Corner · PEATLANDS PK. · M1 · Lurgan · Dolli
A4 · A5 · Eglish · A29 · ARDRESS HOUSE (NT) · A4 · Craigavon · A26 · Ga
Augher · A28 · Carnteel · Moy · THE ARGORY (NT) · Scotch Street · Waringstown · Bleary
ogher · Aughnacloy · Benburb · Charlemont · Cox's Hill · Portadown
Crilly · Dyan · Blackwatertown · Loughgall · Ballyleny · A50
Carrickroe · N2 · Caledon · BENBURB VALLEY · Richhill · Laurelvale · Lawre
Emyvale · CATH (R.C.) · NAVAN FORT · Hamilton's Bawn · Tandragee · A51 · Gilford · Se
Tedavnet · Killylea · ST. PATRICK'S TRIAN · Armagh · A51 · Clare · Scarva · SCARVA VISITOR CEN.
Glaslough · Tynan · Millford · PALACE STABLES HERITAGE CEN · Loughbrickland · Ann
cotstown · CASTLE LESLIE · Middletown · A3 · Markethill · Acton · Mo
Bellanode · COUNTY MUS · N12 · Tyholland · Tassagh · Clady Milltown · Mount Norris · Poyntz Pass · A1
Monaghan (Muineachán) · Castleshane · Keady · Glenanne · A28 · Milltow
Smithborough · Darkley · Carrigatuke 367 · Whitecross · Lurganare · R
Three Mile House · Clontibret · Cavanagarven · Bessbrook · A25

# Belfast information

## General information

Population 341,877. The capital of Northern Ireland. Sited on the River Lagan at the head of Belfast Lough, the city grew from a small village during the industrial revolution with industries such as linen, rope making and shipbuilding.

## Tourist information

The **Belfast Welcome Centre** at 9 Donegall Square North, Belfast BT1 5GJ
☎ 028 9024 6609 www.visitbelfast.com provides an information and accommodation booking service.

The Northern Ireland Tourist Board website is available at www.discovernorthernireland.com

## Getting around

Two bus services run in and around Belfast city. Ulsterbus transports people in and out of the city and serves all major towns and villages. Metro runs around the city, departing and terminating in the city centre. For information on Metro, Ulsterbus and Northern Ireland Railways contact **Translink** ☎ 028 9066 6630 www.translink.co.uk

The main railway station in Belfast is Central Station, East Bridge Street.
For rail enquiries contact **Translink** ☎ 028 9066 6630 www.translink.co.uk

## Places of interest

Queen's University        Photo © Northern Ireland Tourist Board

Buildings of architectural interest include **Belfast City Hall** which dominates Donegall Square. It is a striking classical Renaissance style building completed in 1906 and its great copper dome is a landmark throughout the city. Nearby, the **Linen Hall Library** is Belfast's oldest library and is the leading centre for Irish and local studies in Northern Ireland. Specialising in Irish culture and politics, it also has a unique collection of early printed books from Belfast and Ulster. At Queen's University the **Queen's Welcome Centre** provides information about the university and presents a varied programme of exhibitions. Located at the heart of the campus in the Lanyon Room, the centre is named after Charles Lanyon who was the architect of the main Queen's building and many other public buildings in Ireland. A new iconic building in the heart of Belfast's docklands, **Titanic Belfast** provides visitors with a unique insight into all things Titanic. It tells the story of Titanic from her construction in Belfast to her fateful maiden voyage using stunning special effects, innovative interactive features and full-scale reconstructions.

The extravagant **Crown Liquor Saloon** on Great Victoria Street is of historic interest. It dates from Victorian times and is one of the most famous public houses in Belfast. More recent attractions include **The Odyssey Complex**, a multi-functional entertainment centre which includes a 10,000 seat arena, the W5 interactive discovery centre, cinema and leisure complex. Another well known city centre attraction are the colourful hand painted political murals of West Belfast. They adorn the walls and gable ends of many houses expressing the political viewpoints of the Protestant Shankill Road and the Catholic Falls Road and have become just as much a part of the tourist industry as the more traditional sites of the city. Black cab tours, with commentaries and photo stops, are available to view them.

To the north is **Belfast Castle** which overlooks the city from 122m (400ft) above sea level. Completed in 1870 by the 3rd Marquis of Donegall, this magnificent sandstone castle was refurbished over a 10 year period by

Belfast City Council at a cost of more than £2m and was reopened to the public in 1988. East of the city is **Stormont Parliament Buildings**, the home of the Northern Ireland Parliament. The Main Hall is open to the public and tours for groups can be arranged in advance.

# Theatres, concert halls & festivals

**Belfast Waterfront Hall** ☎ 028 9033 4455 is Northern Ireland's premier concert and conference centre which covers a wide variety of entertainment in its flagship building. The **Grand Opera House** on Great Victoria Street ☎ 028 9024 1919 stages opera, drama, musicals, concerts and pantomime. The declining opulence of the building was restored in 1980 to transform it into a modern theatre whilst still retaining its lavish Victorian interior. **Ulster Hall** ☎ 028 9033 4455, first built in 1862 on Bedford Street ☎ 028 9033 4455, with its interior dominated by a massive English theatre organ, has been a favourite venue for concerts for over 140 years. The main city centre theatre is the **Lyric Theatre** ☎ 028 9038 1081 which presents both classic and contemporary plays with an emphasis on Irish productions.

Annual events and festivals held in Belfast include the **Belfast International Arts Festival** ☎ 028 9033 2261 which is held in late autumn at the campus of Queen's University and other city venues. Hosting international theatre, dance, music and comedy, it is Ireland's largest arts festival. The **Cathedral Quarter Arts Festival** ☎ 028 9023 2403 is held in May to celebrate the best of the local talent as well as new international work.

# Shopping

The main city centre shopping area is Donegall Place, most of which is pedestrianised. Belfast is also renowned for its selection of malls and shopping centres. **Castle Court Shopping Centre** in Royal Avenue is Northern Ireland's largest shopping centre, with over 70 shops extending over 3.4ha (8.5 acres). Opposite Castle Court is the modern **Smithfield Market** which replaced the old Victorian market destroyed by fire in 1974. The **Spires Centre and Mall** was refurbished in 1992 to become one of Belfast's most attractive buildings and is the place to shop for designer fashion and giftware. Belfast's newest shopping centre is **Victoria Square Shopping Centre**, located in the city's Southern Quarter.

# Parks & gardens

**Ormeau Park** opened in 1871 and is the largest park in the centre of the city. South of the city the **Botanic Gardens** are one of Belfast's most popular parks. The restored Palm House was built in 1840 and is one of the earliest examples of a curved glass and wrought iron glasshouse. North of the city **Belfast Zoo** is set in landscaped parkland on the slopes of Cave Hill. Over 160 species are housed there and the zoo increasingly focuses on wildlife facing extinction so has specialised collections with breeding programmes for endangered species.

Botanic Gardens

Photo © Joy Brown
Used under license from Shutterstock.com

# Telephoning

If telephoning from Great Britain or Northern Ireland use the area code and telephone number. If telephoning from the Republic of Ireland replace 028 with 048 and follow with the required telephone number.

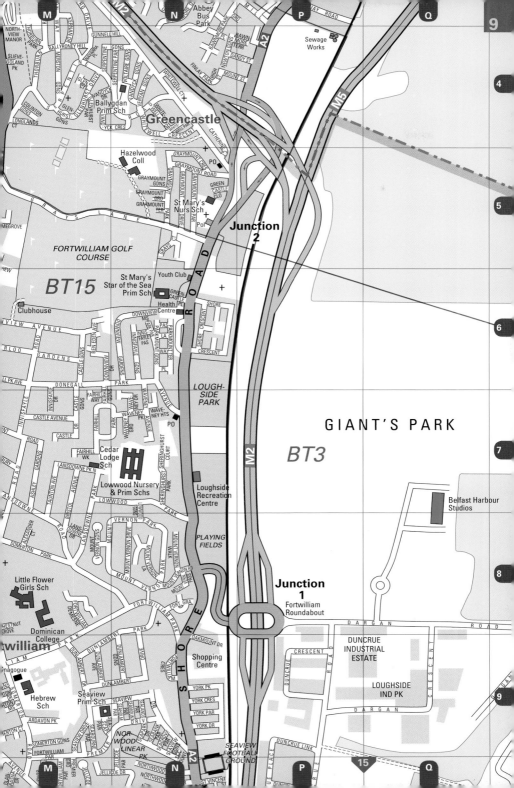

U V W X

4

5

6

7

Cairnryan
Ferry Terminal

BELFAST
HARBOUR
ESTATE

GARMOYLE

WEST ROAD

HERON AVE

BT3

8

Jetty

BELFAST
LOUGH
RESERVE

JETTY ROAD

AIRPORT ROAD

HERON ROAD

15

Observation
Post

9

WORKS

Superstores

A2 R O A

WEST

Holywood
Exchange

Me
Hall

S T

U V W X

16

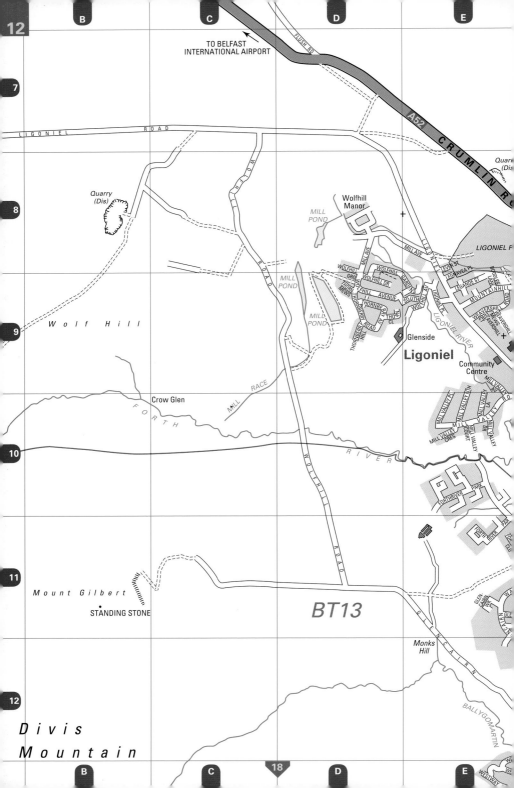

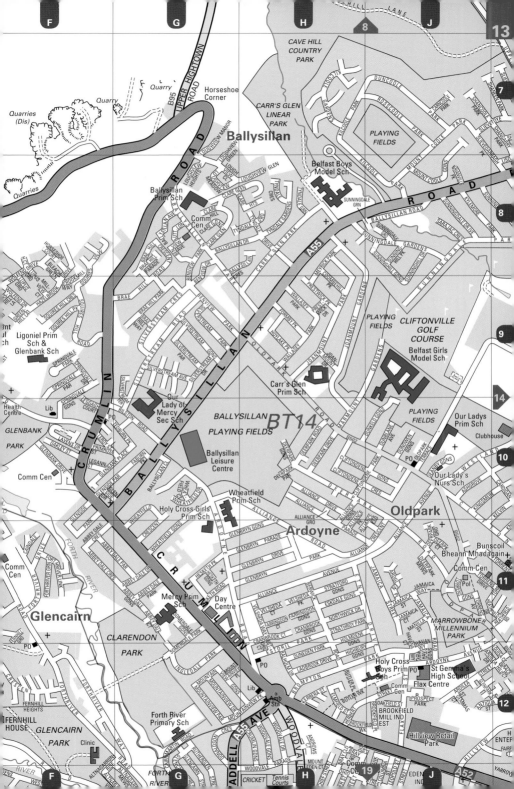

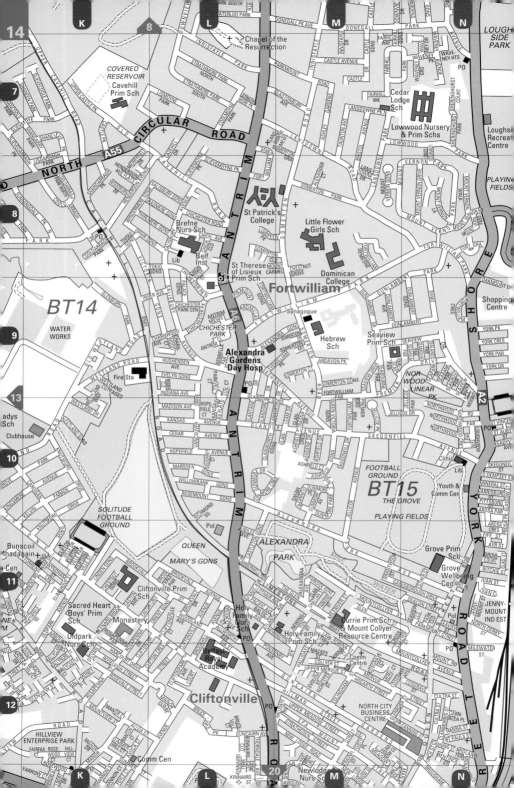

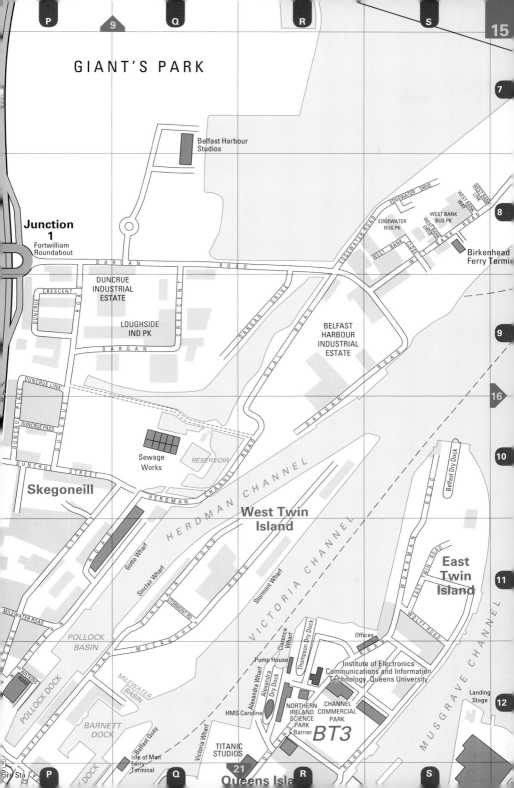

GIANT'S PARK

Belfast Harbour
Studios

**Junction
1**
Fortwilliam
Roundabout

EDGEWATER DRIVE

WEST BANK LINK

EDGEWATER ROAD

WEST BANK
WAY

WEST BANK
BUS PK

WEST BANK
DRIVE

WEST BANK
ROAD

WEST BANK
CLOSE

W

**Birkenhead
Ferry Termi**

DARGAN        ROAD

CRESCENT

DUNCRUE
CRESCENT

DARGAN DRIVE

SEAL ROAD

DARGAN ROAD

DUNCRUE
INDUSTRIAL
ESTATE

LOUGHSIDE
IND PK

DARGAN

DUNCRUE LINK

DUNCRUE PLACE

DUNCRUE PASS

DUNCRUE STREET

DUNCRUE

BELFAST
HARBOUR
INDUSTRIAL
ESTATE

DARGAN

9

16

10

Belfast Dry Dock

Sewage
Works

RESERVOIR

CHANNEL ROAD

**Skegoneill**

HERDMAN

HERDMAN  CHANNEL

**West Twin
Island**

VICTORIA CHANNEL

**East
Twin
Island**

MUSGRAVE CHANNEL

11

12

STREET

SINCLAIR    ROAD

MILEWATER ROAD

Gotto Wharf

Sinclair Wharf

STORMONT RD

ROAD

ROAD

Stormont Wharf

WORKMAN ROAD

EAST TWIN ROAD

WOLF ROAD

INCRUE

RITHER N

WATKINS
ROAD

MCCAUGHEY

Offices

Institute of Electronics
Communications and Information
Technology, Queens University

**POLLOCK
BASIN**

ROAD

MILEWATER
BASIN

Clarence
Wharf

Thompson Dry Dock

**POLLOCK DOCK**

DUFFERIN

Pump House

Alexandra
Dry Dock

Alexandra Wharf

**NORTHERN
IRELAND
SCIENCE
PARK**

**CHANNEL
COMMERCIAL
PARK**

Landing
Stage

**BARNETT
DOCK**

HMS Caroline

Belfast Quay

Isle of Man
Ferry
Terminal

Victoria Wharf

Barrier

**BT3**

QUEENS ROAD

**TITANIC
STUDIOS**

Fire Sta

T　　U　　10　　V　　W

7

Cairnryan
Ferry Terminal

GARMOYLE

BELFAST
HARBOUR
ESTATE

8

WEST BANK LINK

Birkenhead
Ferry Terminal

Jetty

BELFAST
LOUGH
RESERVE

HERON AVE

AIRPORT ROAD WEST

HERON ROAD

BT3

JETTY ROAD

Observation
Post

9

WORKS

15

AIRPORT ROAD WEST

MOSCOW ROAD

10

THE
TILLYSBURN
URBAN
WILDLIFE
RESERVE

DEPOT ROAD

Superstor

A55

GEORGE BEST

BELFAST CITY

AIRPORT

P

BLANCHFLOWER
PARK

Glendhu
Nurs Sch

B505

11

CHANNEL

Terminal
Building

P

FOOTBALL
GRD

GLENDHU

ROAD

MARMON

anding

Jetty

12

Bathing

AIRCRAFT
PARK

HOLYWOOD

MARMONT

Mitc
Hou
Specia

ALDERMAN
TOMMY PATTON
MEMORIAL PARK
(INVERARY
PLAYING FIELDS)

Joss Cardwell
Centre

MARMONT CRES

T　　U　　22　　V　　W

A55

ORTS
GRD

X   Y   Z   AA

BARRA

SPAFIELD PLAYING FIELDS

St Patrick's Prim Sch

KERR PARK

CRAIGTARA

Intergrated College

NORWOOD

Hollywood Adult Ed Cen

PALACE BARRACKS

BELFAST

JACKSONS ROAD

HOLYWOOD ROAD

STRATHEARN COURT

B169

Sacred Heart of Mary Convent

Sullivan Upr Prep School

ABBEY RING

PRIORY END

SOUTH

WEST

THE GREEN

PRIOR

ABBOTS WOOD

Sullivan Upper School

THE GROVE

PO

ABBOTS WOOD

Winshill

WOOD EVU

NUN'S WALK

PINE CREST

HOLYWOOD GOLF COURSE

7

Comm Cen

ARDNAGREENA GDNS

CHURCH

AVE

LARCH CL

DEMESNE

8

Clubhou

Ho

PALACE BARRACKS

Superstores

A2 ROAD

BELFAST

Government Offices

Mertoun Hall

wood ange

HOLYWOOD ROAD

Health Clinic

Redburn Prim Sch

CLARE HILL LA

FIRMOUNT

PALACE GROVE

CRESCENT

HOLYWOOD

Redburn

PLAYING FIELD

Ardtullagh

Club House

CEMETERY

BT18

9

P

REDBURN COUNTRY PARK

HOLYWOOD

10

RORYS WOOD

P

GROVE

CEDAR

Barn End

erstore

RICHMOND MEWS

RICHMOND CT

BENDER

SON CT

ORCHARD

RICHMOND CLO

RICHMOND

AVE

GLENDARRAGH

GONEY PARK

SCHOOL

PO

Comm Cen

KNOCKNAGONEY

AVE

SLUGG

KNOCK-NAGONEY

GRO

Knocknagoney Prim Sch

HOLYWOOD

HOLYWOOD

11

Knocknagoney

GLENLEA PK

GLENLUCE GRN

GARNERVILLE

CARNERVILLE

VILLE PK

GLENMILLAN DR

GLENMILLAN

Glenmachan Tower

Northern Ireland Police College

Youth Club

QUARRY

Quarry (Dis)

BT4

Mo Pa

SCAW

MOSS ROAD

QUARRY ROAD

PARKWAY

GLEN MACHAN ROAD

12

GLEN

BRIDGE

23

omme Home

X   Y   Z   AA

Kileen House

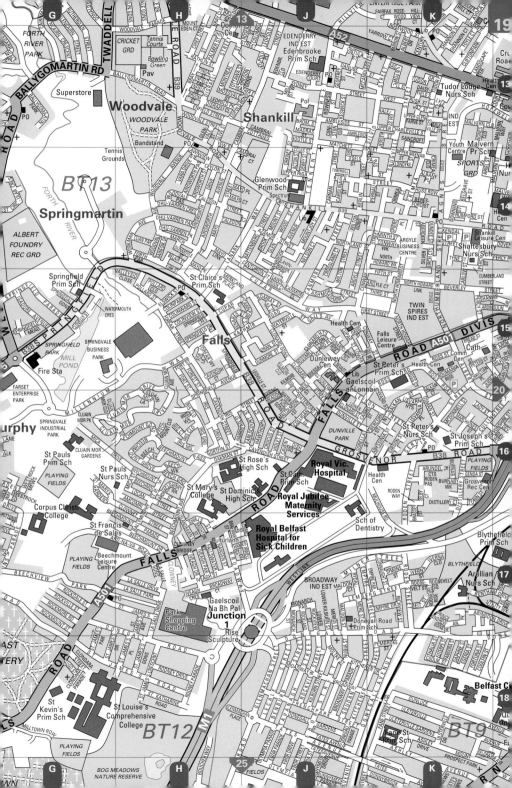

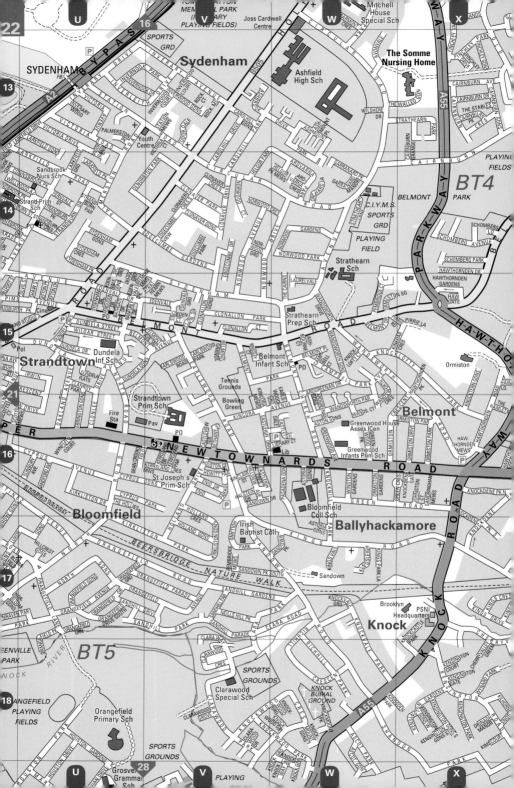

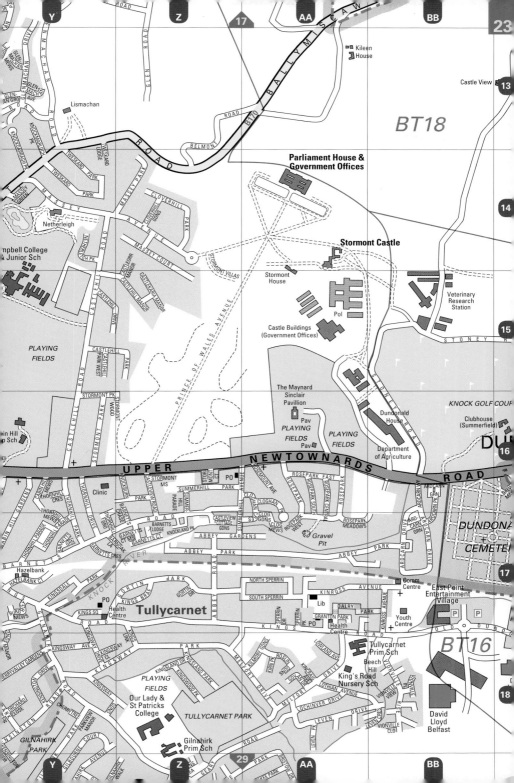

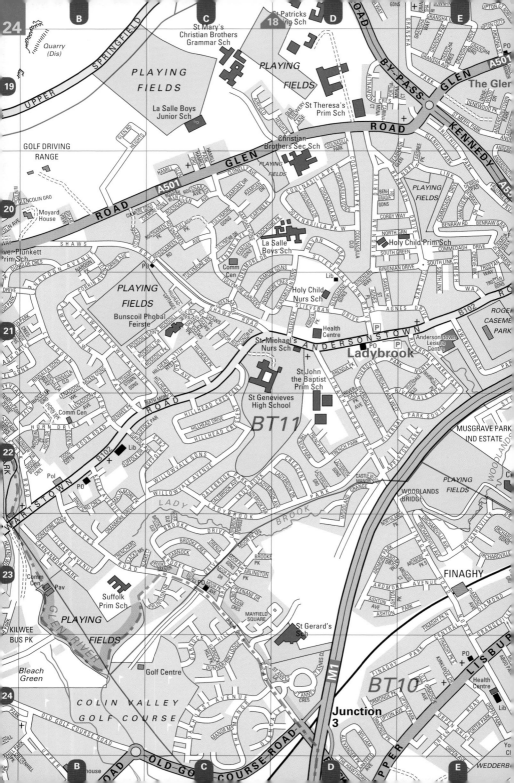

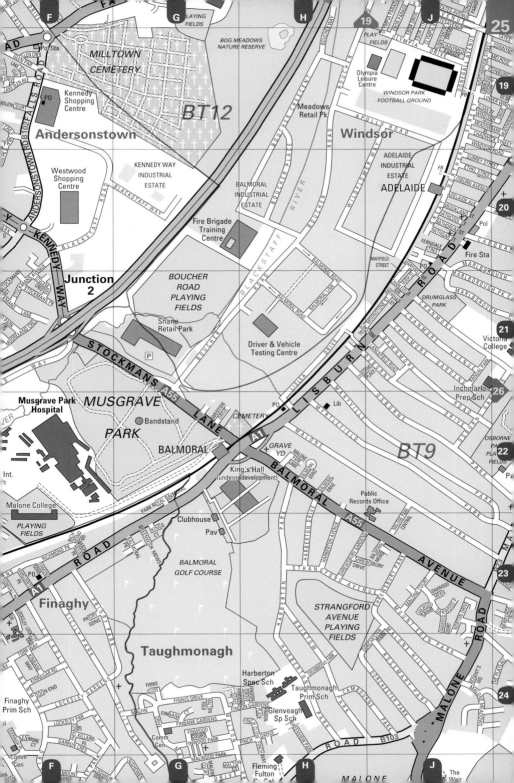

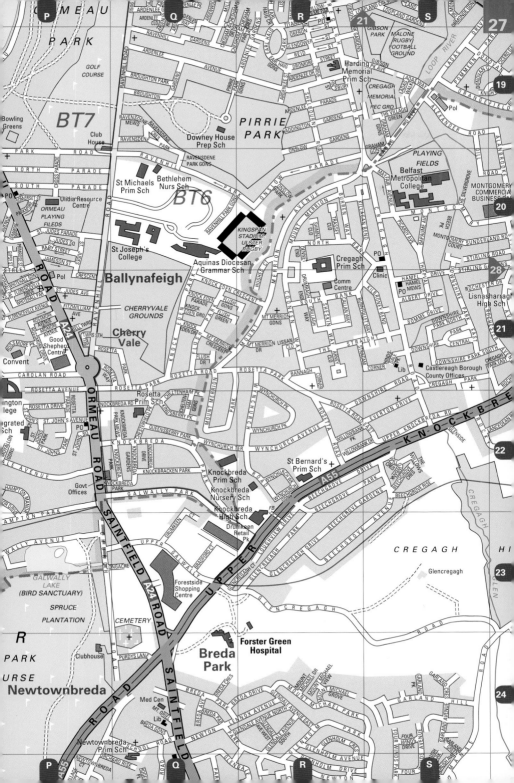

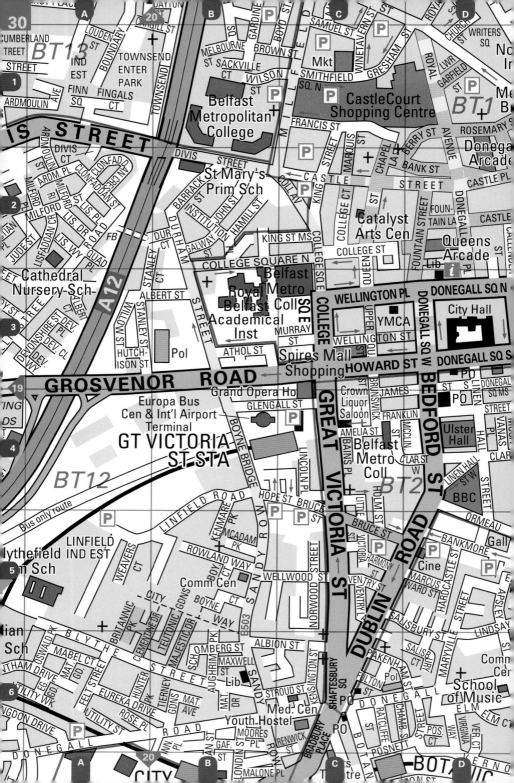

# Index to place names

# Index to street names

## General Abbreviations

| | | | | | | | |
|---|---|---|---|---|---|---|---|
| All | Alley | Dr | Drive | Mkt | Market | Ter | Terrace |
| Arc | Arcade | E | East | Ms | Mews | Vills | Villas |
| Av | Avenue | Embk | Embankment | Mt | Mount | Vw | View |
| Bk | Bank | Fm | Farm | N | North | W | West |
| Bri | Bridge | Gdns | Gardens | Par | Parade | Wd | Wood |
| Cen | Centre, Central | Gra | Grange | Pas | Passage | Wf | Wharf |
| Ch | Church | Grd | Ground | Pk | Park | Wk | Walk |
| Circ | Circus | Grn | Green | Pl | Place | | |
| Clo | Close | Gro | Grove | Rd | Road | | |
| Cor | Corner | Ho | House | Ri | Rise | | |
| Cotts | Cottages | Hts | Heights | S | South | | |
| Cres | Crescent | La | Lane | Sq | Square | | |
| Ct | Court | Lo | Lodge | St. | Saint | | |
| Cts | Courts | Lwr | Lower | St | Street | | |

## Post Town Abbreviations

| | | | |
|---|---|---|---|
| Hol. | Holywood | New. | Newtownabbey |

## Notes

The index contains some roads for which there is insufficient space to name on the map. The adjoining, or nearest named thoroughfare to such roads is shown in *italics*, and the reference indicates where the unnamed road is located off the named thoroughfare.

### A

| | | | | | | | | |
|---|---|---|---|---|---|---|---|---|
| Abbey Ct BT5 | | | Adelaide Chase BT9 | 26 | K20 | Albert Dr BT6 | 27 | S21 | Altigarron Ct BT12 | | |
| *off Abbey Gdns* | 23 | AA17 | Adelaide Pk BT9 | 26 | K20 | Albert Sq BT1 | 20 | N14 | *off Westrock Gdns* | 19 | G16 |
| Abbey Dale Ct BT14 | 13 | G11 | Adelaide St BT2 | 30 | D3 | Albert St BT12 | 30 | A3 | Altnagarron Cl BT13 | 19 | G13 |
| Abbey Dale Cres BT14 | 13 | F11 | Adela Pl BT14 | 20 | L13 | Albert Ter BT12 | | | Altnagarron Ms BT13 | 19 | G13 |
| Abbey Dale Dr BT14 | 13 | G11 | Adela St BT14 | 20 | L13 | *off Albert St* | 19 | K15 | Altnagarron Ri BT13 | 18 | F13 |
| Abbey Dale Gdns | | | Advantage Way BT13 | 18 | F14 | Albertville Dr BT14 | 19 | K13 | Altnagarron Vw BT13 | 18 | F13 |
| BT14 | 13 | G11 | Agincourt Av BT7 | 26 | M19 | Albion La BT7 | | | Alton St BT13 | 20 | M14 |
| Abbey Dale Par BT14 | 13 | F11 | Agincourt St BT7 | 20 | N18 | *off Bradbury Pl* | 30 | C6 | Ambleside Ct BT13 | 19 | J13 |
| Abbey Dale Pk BT14 | 13 | G11 | Agnes Cl BT13 | 19 | K13 | Albion St BT12 | 30 | B6 | Ambleside St BT13 | 19 | J13 |
| Abbey Gdns BT5 | 23 | Z17 | Agnes St BT13 | 19 | K14 | Alder Cl BT5 | 29 | Y19 | Amcomri St BT12 | 19 | H16 |
| Abbey Pk BT5 | 23 | Z17 | Agra St BT7 | 26 | N19 | Alexander Ct BT15 | 9 | M8 | Amelia St BT2 | 30 | C4 |
| Abbey Pl, Hol. BT18 | | | Aigburth Pk BT4 | 21 | T15 | Alexander Rd BT6 | 27 | S19 | Ampere St BT6 | 21 | Q18 |
| *off Abbey Ring* | 11 | Z7 | Ailesbury Cres BT7 | 26 | N21 | Alexandra Av BT15 | 14 | M11 | Anderson Ct BT5 | 21 | Q16 |
| Abbey Ring, Hol. BT18 | 11 | Z7 | Ailesbury Dr BT7 | 26 | N21 | Alexandra Gdns BT15 | 14 | L9 | Andersonstown Cres | | |
| Abbey Rd BT5 | 23 | Z17 | Ailesbury Gdns BT7 | 26 | N21 | Alexandra Pk, Hol. | | | BT11 | 24 | E19 |
| Abbey St W BT15 | | | Ailesbury Rd BT7 | 26 | N21 | BT18 | 11 | AA7 | Andersonstown Dr | | |
| *off Hanna St* | 14 | N12 | Ainsworth Av BT13 | 19 | H14 | Alexandra Pk Av BT15 | 14 | L10 | BT11 | 24 | E19 |
| Abbots Wd, Hol. BT18 | 11 | Z8 | Ainsworth Dr BT13 | 19 | H14 | Alexandra Pl, Hol. BT18 | | | Andersonstown Gdns | | |
| Abercorn St BT9 | 20 | L18 | Ainsworth Par BT13 | | | *off Church Vw* | 11 | AA6 | BT11 | 24 | E19 |
| Abercorn St N BT12 | 19 | K16 | *off Vara Dr* | 19 | H14 | Alford Pk BT5 | | | Andersonstown Gro | | |
| Abercorn Wk BT12 | | | Ainsworth Pass BT13 | 19 | H14 | *off Melfort Dr* | 23 | AA18 | BT11 | 24 | E20 |
| *off Abercorn St N* | 19 | K16 | Ainsworth St BT13 | 19 | H14 | Alfred St BT2 | 31 | E3 | Andersonstown Par | | |
| Aberdeen St BT13 | 19 | K14 | Airfield Hts BT11 | 24 | D19 | Alliance Av BT14 | 13 | H11 | BT11 | | |
| Abetta Par BT5 | 21 | S17 | Airport Rd BT3 | 21 | S14 | Alliance Cl BT14 | 13 | H11 | *off Andersonstown* | | |
| Abingdon Dr BT12 | 19 | K17 | Airport Rd W BT3 | 16 | T11 | Alliance Cres BT14 | 13 | H11 | *Gdns* | 24 | E19 |
| Aboo Ct BT10 | 24 | E24 | Aitnamona Cres BT11 | 24 | D19 | Alliance Dr BT14 | 13 | H10 | Andersonstown Pk | | |
| Abyssinia St BT12 | 19 | K16 | Alanbrooke Rd BT6 | 28 | T19 | Alliance Gdns BT14 | 13 | H10 | BT11 | 24 | E19 |
| Abyssinia St BT12 | 19 | K16 | Albany Pl BT13 | 19 | K14 | Alliance Gro BT14 | 13 | H10 | Andersonstown Pk S | | |
| *off Abyssinia St* | 19 | K16 | Albany Sq BT13 | | | Alliance Par BT14 | 13 | H10 | BT11 | 24 | E20 |
| Academy St BT1 | 20 | M14 | *off Crimea St* | 19 | K14 | Alliance Pk BT14 | 13 | H11 | Andersonstown Pk W | | |
| Acton St BT13 | 19 | J14 | Albert Br BT1 | 31 | H3 | Alliance Rd BT14 | 13 | H11 | BT11 | 24 | E19 |
| Adelaide Av BT9 | 25 | J20 | Albert Br BT5 | 31 | H3 | Alloa St BT14 | 14 | K12 | Andersonstown Pl BT11 | | |
| | | | Albertbridge Rd BT5 | 21 | Q16 | Allworthy Av BT14 | 14 | L11 | *off Andersonstown* | | |
| | | | Albert Ct BT12 | 30 | A3 | Altcar Ct BT5 | 21 | Q16 | *Pk* | 25 | F19 |

Andersonstown Rd BT11   24   D21
Andrews Ct BT13   13   H12
Anglesea St BT13
*off Beresford St*   19   K14
Annadale Av BT7   26   N22
Annadale Cres BT7   26   M21
Annadale Dr BT7   26   M21
Annadale Embk BT7   26   M21
Annadale Flats BT7   26   N20
Annadale Gdns BT7   26   N21
Annadale Grn BT7   26   N21
Annadale Gro BT7   26   N21
Annadale Ms BT7   26   N21
Annadale Sq BT7   26   N21
Annadale Ter BT7   26   M21
Annadale Village BT7   26   N21
Annalee Ct BT14
*off Avonbeg Cl*   14   K12
Annesley St BT14   20   L13
Annsboro St BT13
*off Sugarfield St*   19   J14
Ann St BT1   31   E2
Antigua Ct BT14
*off Glenpark St*   14   K12
Antigua St BT14   13   J12
Antrim Cl BT15   14   L9
Antrim Ms BT15   14   L9
Antrim Rd BT15   8   L8
Antrim St BT13   20   L14
Apollo Rd BT12   25   H19
Appleton Pk BT11   24   D22
Apsley St BT7   30   D5
Arbour St BT14   14   K11
Aravon Pk BT15   14   M9
Ardcarn Dr BT5   23   BB17
Ardcarn Grn BT5   23   BB16
Ardcarn Pk BT5   23   BB17
Ardcarn Way BT5   23   BB16
Ardenlee Av BT6   27   Q19
Ardenlee Cl BT6   21   Q18
Ardenlee Ct BT6   21   Q18
Ardenlee Cres BT6   21   Q18
Ardenlee Dr BT6   27   R19
Ardenlee Gdns BT6   21   Q18
Ardenlee Grn BT6   21   Q18
Ardenlee Par BT6   27   R19
Ardenlee Pk BT6   21   Q18
Ardenlee Pl BT6   21   Q18
Ardenlee Ri BT6   27   Q19
Ardenlee St BT6   27   R19
Ardenlee Way BT6   21   Q18
Ardenvohr St BT6   21   R18
Ardenwood BT6   21   Q18
Ardglen Pl BT14   13   J11
Ardgowan Dr BT6   21   S18
Ardgowan St BT6   21   R18
Ardgreenan Cres BT4
*off Campbell Pk Av*   22   W15
Ardgreenan Dr BT4   22   W15
Ardgreenan Gdns BT4   22   W16
Ardgreenan Mt BT4
*off Wandsworth Par*   22   W16
Ardgreenan Pl BT4
*off Wandsworth Par*   22   W16
Ardilaun BT4
*off Lackagh Ct*   21   Q15
Ardilea Ct BT14
*off Ardilea Dr*   13   J12
Ardilea Dr BT14   13   J12
Ardilea St BT14   13   J12
Ardkeen Cres BT6   28   U20
Ardlee Av, Hol. BT18   11   AA7
Ardmillan BT15   14   L9
Ardmonagh Gdns BT11   18   E17
Ardmonagh Par BT11   18   E17
Ardmonagh Way BT11   18   E17
Ardmore Av BT7   27   P21
Ardmore Av, Hol. BT18   11   BB6
Ardmore Ct BT10   24   E23
Ardmore Dr BT10   24   D23
Ardmore Pk BT10   24   D23
Ardmore Pk, Hol. BT18   11   BB6
Ardmore Pk S BT10   24   E23
Ardmore Ter, Hol. BT18   11   BB6
Ardmoulin Av BT13   19   K15

Ardmoulin Cl BT13
*off Ardmoulin Av*   30   A1
Ardmoulin Pl BT12   30   A2
Ardmoulin St BT12   30   A1
Ardmoulin Ter BT12
*off Ardmoulin St*   30   A2
Ardnaclowney Dr BT12   19   H16
Ardnagreena Gdns, Hol. BT18   11   Z8
Ard-na-va Rd BT12   19   G17
Ardoyne Av BT14   13   J12
Ardoyne Ct BT14
*off Ardoyne Av*   13   J12
Ardoyne Pl BT14
*off Ardoyne Av*   13   J12
Ardoyne Rd BT14   13   G10
Ardoyne Sq BT14
*off Ardoyne Av*   13   J11
Ardoyne Wk BT14
*off Ardoyne Av*   13   J12
Ardpatrick Gdns BT6   28   T19
Ardvarna Cres BT4   22   W14
Ardvarna Pk BT4   22   W14
Argyle Ct BT13   19   K15
Argyle St BT13   19   J15
Ariel St BT13   19   K14
Arizona St BT11   24   E19
Arlington Dr BT11   24   C23
Arlington Pk BT10   24   C23
Armitage Cl BT4
*off Harkness Par*   21   S14
Arney Cl BT6   27   R21
Arnon St BT13   20   M14
Arosa Cres BT15   14   N11
Arosa Par BT15   14   N10
Arosa Pk BT15   14   N11
Arran Ct BT5
*off Arran St*   21   Q16
Arran St BT5   21   Q16
Artana St BT7   20   N18
Arthur La BT1   31   E3
Arthur Pl BT1   31   E2
Arthur Sq BT1   31   E2
Arthur St BT1   31   E2
Arundel Cts BT12   19   K16
Arundel Ho BT12
*off Arundel Cts*   19   K16
Arundel Wk BT12
*off Roden Pas*   19   K16
Ascot Gdns BT5   22   W18
Ascot Ms BT5
*off Knockmount Pk*   22   W18
Ascot Pk BT5   22   W18
Ashbourne Ct BT4   22   W15
Ashbrook Cres BT4
*off Ashbrook Dr*   22   W13
Ashbrook Dr BT4   22   V13
Ashburne Ms BT7
*off Salisbury St*   30   D5
Ashburne Pl BT7
*off Salisbury St*   30   D5
Ashburn Grn BT4
*off Ashmount Pk*   22   W13
Ashdale St BT5   21   S16
Ashdene Dr BT15   14   M10
Ashfield Ct BT15   14   M10
Ashfield Cres BT15   14   M10
Ashfield Dr BT15   14   M10
Ashfield Gdns BT15   14   M10
Ashford Grn BT4
*off Ashmount Pk*   22   W13
Ash Grn, Hol. BT18
*off Loughview Av*   11   Z8
Ashgrove Rk BT14   13   J10
Ashleigh Manor BT9   26   K19
Ashley Av BT9   19   K18
Ashley Dr BT9   19   K18
Ashley Gdns BT15   9   M7
Ashley Ms BT9   26   K19
Ashmore Pl BT13   19   J15
Ashmore St BT13   19   J15
Ashmount Gro BT4
*off Ashmount Pk*   22   W13
Ashmount Pk BT4   22   W13
Ashmount Pl BT4   22   W13
Ashton Av BT10   24   D23
Ashton Pk BT10   24   D23
Aston Gdns BT4   22   W16

Astoria Gdns BT5   22   W16
Athol St BT12   30   B3
Athol St La BT12
*off Athol St*   30   B3
Atlantic Av BT15   14   L11
Aughrim Pk BT12   30   B6
Ava Av BT7   26   N20
Ava Cres BT7   26   N21
Ava Dr BT7   26   N20
Ava Gdns BT7   26   N20
Ava Par BT7   26   N20
Ava Pk BT7   26   N20
Ava St BT7   26   N20
Avoca Cl BT11   18   D17
Avoca St BT14   14   K12
Avonbeg Cl BT14   14   K12
Avondale St BT5   21   T16
Avoniel Dr BT5   21   S17
Avoniel Par BT5   21   S17
Avoniel Rd BT5   21   S16
Avonorr Dr BT5   21   S17
Avonvale BT4   22   W13
Ayr St BT15   14   N11
Azamor St BT13   19   J14

**B**

Back Mt St BT5   21   Q16
Baden Powell St BT13   19   K13
Bainesmore Dr BT13   19   H14
Bains Pl BT2   30   C4
Balfour Av BT7   20   P18
Balholm Dr BT14   13   H12
Balkan Ct BT12   19   K15
Balkan St BT12   19   K16
Ballaghbeg BT11
*off Bearnagh Dr*   24   D20
Ballarat Ct BT6   20   Q17
Ballarat St BT6   31   H5
Ballycarry St BT14
*off Ballynure St*   14   K12
Ballycastle Ct BT14   14   K12
Ballycastle St BT14
*off Ballynure St*   14   K12
Ballyclare Ct BT14   14   K12
Ballyclare St BT14
*off Ballynure St*   14   K12
Ballyclare Way BT14
*off Ballynure St*   14   K12
Ballygomartin Dr BT13   18   F14
Ballygomartin Pk BT13   19   G13
Ballygomartin Rd BT13   18   D15
Ballygowan Rd BT5   28   V20
Ballyhanwood Rd BT5   29   AA20
Ballymacarrett Rd BT4   21   Q15
Ballymacarrett Walkway BT4
*off Dee St*   21   S15
Ballymagarry La BT13   18   E14
Ballymena BT14
*off Ballymoney St*   14   K12
Ballymenoch Pk, Hol. BT18   11   BB4
Ballymiscaw Rd, Hol. BT18   23   AA13
Ballymoney Ct BT14
*off Ballymoney St*   14   K12
Ballymoney St BT14   14   K12
Ballymurphy Cres BT12   18   E16
Ballymurphy Dr BT12   18   F16
Ballymurphy Par BT12   18   E16
Ballymurphy Rd BT12   18   F16
Ballymurphy St BT12   19   H17
Ballynure St BT14   14   K12
Ballynure Way BT14
*off Ballynure St*   14   K12
Ballyroney Hill, New. BT36   9   M4
Ballysillan Av BT14   13   G8
Ballysillan Cl BT14   13   G10
Ballysillan Cres BT14   13   G8
Ballysillan Dr BT14   13   G8
Ballysillan Pk BT14   13   G8
Ballysillan Rd BT14   13   G10
Balmoral Av BT9   25   H22
Balmoral Ct BT9
*off Lisburn Rd*   25   G22
Balmoral Dr BT9   25   H22

Balmoral Gdns BT9   25   H22
Balmoral Link BT12   25   H21
Balmoral Ms BT9   25   J23
Balmoral Pk (Finaghy) BT10   25   G23
Balmoral Rd BT12   25   H20
Baltic Av BT15   14   L11
Bandon Ct BT14   14   K12
Bangor Rd, Hol. BT18   11   AA5
Bankmore Sq BT7
*off Bankmore St*   30   D5
Bankmore St BT7   30   D5
Bank St BT1   30   C2
Bannagh Cor BT6   27   R21
Bann Ct BT14
*off Shannon St*   19   K13
Bantry St BT13
*off Kashmir Rd*   19   J15
Bapaume Av BT6   27   S20
Barnetts Chase BT5   23   Z17
Barnetts Ct BT5   23   Z17
Barnetts Ct Ms BT5   23   Y17
Barnetts Cres BT5   23   Y17
Barnetts Grn BT5   23   Y17
Barnetts Lo BT5   23   Z17
Barnetts Rd BT5   23   Y17
Barnoak La BT5   23   Z17
Baroda Dr BT7   26   N19
Baroda Par BT7   26   N19
Baroda St BT7   26   N19
Barrack St BT12   30   B2
Barrington Gdns BT12
*off Abingdon Dr*   19   K17
Baskin St BT5   21   R15
Bathgate Dr BT4   22   U15
Batley St BT5   21   T16
Battenberg Ct BT13
*off Battenberg St*   19   H14
Battenberg St BT13   19   J14
Bawnmore Ct BT9
*off Bawnmore Rd*   25   J21
Bawnmore Pk, New. BT36
*off Newton Gdns*   9   N4
Bawnmore Rd BT9   25   J21
Bawnmore Ter, New. BT36   9   N4
Bearnagh Dr BT11   24   D20
Bearnagh Glen BT11
*off Bearnagh Dr*   24   D20
Bedford Sq BT2   30   D4
Bedford St BT2   30   D3
Beech End, Hol. BT18   11   Z8
Beeches, The BT7
*off Hampton Pk*   26   N22
Beechfield Ct BT5
*off Beechfield St*   21   R15
Beechfield St BT5   21   Q16
Beechgrove Av BT6   27   R23
Beechgrove Cres BT6   27   S22
Beechgrove Dr BT6   27   R22
Beechgrove Gdns BT6   27   R23
Beechgrove Pk BT6   27   R22
Beechgrove Ri BT6   27   S22
Beech Hts BT7   26   N22
Beechlands BT9   26   L20
Beechmount Av BT12   19   H17
Beechmount Cl BT12   19   H16
Beechmount Cres BT12   19   H16
Beechmount Dr BT12   19   H17
Beechmount Gdns BT12   19   H16
Beechmount Gro BT12   19   H16
Beechmount Link BT12   19   H16
Beechmount Par BT12   19   G16
Beechmount Pk BT10   25   F23
Beechmount Pass BT12   19   H16
Beechmount St BT12   19   H16
Beechmount Wk BT12   19   H16
Beechnut Pl BT14
*off Oldpark Rd*   14   K12
Beech Pk BT6   28   T20
Beechpark St BT14
*off Oldpark Rd*   14   K12
Beechview Pk BT12   19   G17

| Street | Pg | Grid |
|---|---|---|
| Beechwood St BT5 | 21 | T16 |
| Beersbridge Rd BT5 | 21 | R17 |
| Beit St BT12 | 19 | K17 |
| Belair St BT13 | 19 | H14 |
| Belfast Rd, Hol. BT18 | 16 | W10 |
| Belgrave St BT13 | 19 | K14 |
| Belgravia Av BT9 | 19 | K18 |
| Bellbashford Ct BT6 | | |
| *off Woodstock Pl* | 21 | Q16 |
| Bell Cl BT13 | | |
| *off Bootle St* | 19 | J13 |
| Bellfield Hts BT12 | 18 | D17 |
| Bell Twrs BT7 | 27 | P21 |
| Bell Twrs S BT7 | 27 | P21 |
| Belmont Av BT4 | 22 | U15 |
| Belmont Av W BT4 | 22 | V15 |
| Belmont Ch Rd BT4 | 22 | W15 |
| Belmont Cl BT4 | | |
| *off Belmont Av* | 22 | V15 |
| Belmont Ct BT4 | | |
| *off Sydenham Av* | 22 | V15 |
| Belmont Dr BT4 | 22 | W15 |
| Belmont Gra BT4 | 22 | V15 |
| Belmont Ms BT4 | 22 | U15 |
| Belmont Pk BT4 | 22 | V15 |
| Belmont Pl BT4 | 22 | W15 |
| Belmont Rd BT4 | 22 | U15 |
| Belvedere Manor BT9 | 26 | K20 |
| Belvedere Pk BT9 | 26 | M22 |
| Belvoir St BT5 | 21 | R15 |
| Benares St BT13 | 19 | H15 |
| Benbradagh Gdns BT11 | 24 | D20 |
| Benburb St BT12 | 19 | J18 |
| Bendigo St BT6 | 21 | Q17 |
| Ben Eden Av BT15 | 9 | M6 |
| Ben Eden Ct BT15 | | |
| *off Ben Eden Av* | 9 | M6 |
| Ben Eden Grn BT15 | | |
| *off Ben Eden Av* | 9 | M6 |
| Ben Eden Pk BT15 | | |
| *off Ben Eden Av* | 9 | M6 |
| Ben Madigan Pk, New. BT36 | 8 | L4 |
| Ben Madigan Pk S, New. BT36 | 8 | L4 |
| Benmore Ct BT10 | 25 | F24 |
| Benmore Dr BT10 | 25 | F24 |
| Bennett Dr BT14 | | |
| *off Brookvale Av* | 14 | L11 |
| Benraw Gdns BT11 | | |
| *off Benraw Rd* | | |
| Benraw Grn BT11 | 24 | E20 |
| Benraw Rd BT11 | 24 | E20 |
| Benraw Ter BT11 | | |
| *off Benraw Rd* | 24 | E20 |
| Bentham Dr BT4 | 19 | K17 |
| Bentinck St BT15 | 14 | N12 |
| Benview Av BT14 | 13 | G8 |
| Benview Dr BT14 | 13 | G9 |
| Benview Pk BT14 | 13 | G9 |
| Benwee Pk BT11 | 24 | B22 |
| Beresford St BT13 | 19 | K14 |
| Berkeley Rd BT3 | 20 | P13 |
| Berlin St BT13 | 19 | J14 |
| Berry St BT1 | 30 | D2 |
| Berwick Rd BT14 | 13 | H11 |
| Bethany St BT4 | 22 | V16 |
| Beverley St BT13 | 19 | K15 |
| Bilston Rd BT14 | 13 | G10 |
| Bingnian Dr BT11 | 24 | D20 |
| Bingnian Way BT11 | 24 | D21 |
| Birch Dr, Hol. BT18 | 11 | AA6 |
| Black Mountain Gro BT13 | 18 | F15 |
| Black Mountain Par BT13 | 18 | F15 |
| Black Mountain Pk BT13 | 18 | F15 |
| Black Mountain Pl BT13 | 18 | F15 |
| Black Mountain Wk BT13 | 18 | F14 |
| Black Mountain Way BT13 | 18 | F15 |
| Blacks Ct BT11 | 24 | B23 |
| Blacks Ms BT11 | 24 | B23 |
| Blacks Rd BT10 | 24 | C23 |
| Blacks Rd BT11 | 24 | B23 |
| Blackstaff Rd BT11 | 25 | F20 |
| Blackstaff Way BT11 | 25 | G20 |
| Blackwater Way BT12 | | |
| *off Brassey St* | 19 | K17 |
| Blackwood St BT7 | 26 | N20 |
| Bladon Ct BT9 | 26 | L23 |
| Bladon Dr BT9 | 26 | K22 |
| Bladon Pk BT9 | 26 | K22 |
| Blakeley Ter BT12 | | |
| *off Rowland Way* | 30 | B5 |
| Blaney St BT13 | | |
| *off Crimea St* | 19 | K13 |
| Bleach Grn BT14 | 13 | F8 |
| Bleach Grn Ct BT12 | 18 | E17 |
| Bleach Grn Ter BT12 | | |
| *off Whiterock Gro* | 18 | E17 |
| Blenheim Dr BT6 | 28 | T19 |
| Blondin St BT12 | 20 | L18 |
| Bloomdale St BT5 | 21 | T16 |
| Bloomfield Av BT5 | 21 | T16 |
| Bloomfield Ct BT5 | 21 | S16 |
| Bloomfield Cres BT5 | 21 | S16 |
| Bloomfield Dr BT5 | 21 | S16 |
| Bloomfield Gdns BT5 | 21 | T17 |
| Bloomfield Par BT5 | 21 | S16 |
| Bloomfield Pk BT5 | 21 | T17 |
| Bloomfield Pk W BT5 | 21 | T17 |
| Bloomfield Rd BT5 | 21 | T16 |
| Bloomfield St BT5 | 21 | S16 |
| Blythe St BT12 | 30 | A6 |
| Bombay St BT13 | 19 | J15 |
| Bond St BT7 | 31 | F5 |
| Boodles Hill BT14 | | |
| *off Mountainhill Rd* | 12 | E9 |
| Boodles La BT14 | 12 | E8 |
| Bootle St BT13 | 19 | J13 |
| Botanic Av BT7 | 30 | C6 |
| Botanic Ct BT7 | | |
| *off Agincourt Av* | 26 | M19 |
| Boucher Cres BT12 | 25 | H19 |
| Boucher Pl BT12 | 25 | H20 |
| Boucher Rd BT9 | 25 | G21 |
| Boucher Rd BT12 | 25 | G21 |
| Boucher Way BT12 | 25 | H19 |
| Boulevard, The BT7 | 26 | N21 |
| Boundary St BT13 | 20 | A1 |
| Boundary Wk BT13 | 20 | L14 |
| Boundary Way BT13 | 20 | L14 |
| Bowness St BT13 | 19 | J13 |
| Boyd St BT13 | 30 | B1 |
| Boyne Br BT12 | 30 | B4 |
| Boyne Ct BT12 | 30 | B5 |
| Bradbury Pl BT7 | 20 | M18 |
| Bradford Pl BT8 | | |
| *off Church Rd* | 27 | P23 |
| Bradford Sq BT1 | | |
| *off Steam Mill La* | 20 | N14 |
| Bradys La BT13 | | |
| *off Boundary St* | 20 | L14 |
| Brae Hill Cres BT14 | 13 | G8 |
| Brae Hill Link BT14 | | |
| *off Brae Hill Rd* | 13 | G9 |
| Brae Hill Par BT14 | 13 | G8 |
| Brae Hill Rd BT14 | 13 | G9 |
| Brae Hill Way BT14 | 13 | G9 |
| Braemar St BT12 | 19 | H17 |
| Braeside Gro BT5 | 28 | W20 |
| Bramcote St BT5 | 21 | T17 |
| Brandon Par BT4 | 21 | T14 |
| Brandon Ter BT4 | 21 | T15 |
| Brandra St BT4 | 21 | T15 |
| Braniel Cres BT5 | 28 | W20 |
| Braniel Pk BT5 | 28 | W20 |
| Braniel Way BT5 | 28 | W20 |
| Brantwood St BT15 | 14 | M11 |
| Brassey St BT12 | 19 | K17 |
| Bray Cl BT13 | 13 | H12 |
| Bray Ct BT13 | | |
| *off Bray Cl* | 13 | H12 |
| Bray St BT13 | 19 | H13 |
| Breach Cl BT5 | | |
| *off Clandeboye St* | 21 | R16 |
| Bread St BT12 | 19 | K15 |
| Breda Av BT8 | 27 | Q24 |
| Breda Cres BT8 | 27 | Q24 |
| Breda Dr BT8 | 27 | Q24 |
| Breda Gdns BT8 | 27 | Q24 |
| Breda Par BT8 | 27 | Q24 |
| Breda Pk BT8 | 27 | Q24 |
| Brenda Pk BT11 | 24 | D21 |
| Brenda St BT5 | 21 | S17 |
| Brentwood Pk BT5 | 28 | V20 |
| Brianville Pk BT14 | 8 | J8 |
| Briar Vw BT11 | 24 | B20 |
| Briarwood Pk BT5 | 29 | Z19 |
| Bridge End BT5 | 31 | G2 |
| Bridge End Flyover BT4 | 21 | Q15 |
| Bridge End Flyover BT5 | 21 | Q15 |
| Bridge St BT1 | 31 | E1 |
| Brighton St BT13 | 19 | H17 |
| Bright St BT5 | | |
| *off Hornby St* | 21 | R16 |
| Bristol Av BT15 | | M7 |
| Bristow Dr BT5 | 29 | AA19 |
| Bristow Pk BT9 | 25 | H23 |
| Britannic Dr BT12 | | |
| *off Rowland Way* | 30 | B5 |
| Britannic Rd BT12 | 30 | A6 |
| Britannic Ter BT12 | | |
| *off Rowland Way* | 30 | B5 |
| Brittons Ct BT12 | 19 | G17 |
| Brittons Dr BT12 | 18 | F17 |
| Brittons Par BT12 | 19 | G17 |
| Broadway BT12 | 19 | H17 |
| Broadway Ct BT12 | | |
| *off Iveagh Cres* | 19 | H17 |
| Broadway Par BT12 | 19 | J18 |
| Bromfield BT9 | 26 | K20 |
| Bromley St BT13 | 19 | J13 |
| Brompton Pk BT14 | 13 | H12 |
| Brooke Cl BT11 | 24 | C23 |
| Brooke Ct BT11 | 24 | C23 |
| Brooke Cres BT11 | 24 | C23 |
| Brooke Dr BT11 | 24 | C23 |
| Brooke Manor BT11 | 24 | C23 |
| Brooke Pk BT10 | 24 | C23 |
| Brookfield Pl BT14 | 13 | J12 |
| Brookfield St BT14 | | |
| *off Herbert St* | 13 | J12 |
| Brookfield Wk BT14 | 13 | H12 |
| Brookhill Av BT14 | 14 | L12 |
| Brookland St BT9 | 25 | J20 |
| Brook Meadow BT5 | 29 | Z19 |
| Brookmill Way BT14 | 13 | F9 |
| Brookmount Gdns BT13 | | |
| *off Lawnbrook Av* | 19 | J14 |
| Brookmount St BT13 | 19 | J14 |
| Brook St, Hol. BT18 | 11 | AA6 |
| Brookvale Av BT14 | 14 | L11 |
| Brookvale Dr BT14 | 14 | L11 |
| Brookvale Par BT14 | 14 | L11 |
| Brookvale St BT14 | 14 | K11 |
| Brookville St BT14 | 14 | L11 |
| Broomhill Cl BT9 | 26 | K22 |
| Broomhill St BT9 | 26 | K22 |
| Broomhill Manor BT9 | | |
| *off Stranmillis Rd* | 26 | K22 |
| Broomhill Pk BT9 | 26 | K22 |
| Broomhill Pk Cen BT9 | 26 | L22 |
| Broom St BT12 | 19 | H13 |
| Brougham St BT15 | 14 | N12 |
| Broughton Gdns BT6 | 27 | Q19 |
| Broughton Pk BT6 | 27 | Q19 |
| Brown Sq BT13 | 20 | L14 |
| Browns Row BT1 | | |
| *off Academy St* | 20 | N14 |
| Brown St BT13 | 30 | B1 |
| Bruce St BT2 | 30 | C4 |
| Brucevale Ct BT14 | 14 | L12 |
| Brucevale Pk BT14 | 14 | L12 |
| Brunswick St BT2 | 30 | C3 |
| Bruslee Way BT15 | 20 | M13 |
| Brussels St BT13 | 19 | J14 |
| Bryansford Pl BT6 | 21 | R17 |
| Bryson Ct BT5 | | |
| *off Mountforde Rd* | 21 | Q15 |
| Bryson Gdns BT5 | | |
| *off Mountforde Rd* | 21 | Q15 |
| Bryson St BT5 | 21 | Q15 |
| Burghley Ms BT5 | 23 | Y17 |
| Burmah St BT7 | 26 | N19 |
| Burnaby Ct BT12 | | |
| *off Distillery St* | 19 | K16 |
| Burnaby Pk BT12 | | |
| *off Distillery St* | 19 | K16 |
| Burnaby Pl BT12 | 19 | K16 |
| Burnaby Wk BT12 | 19 | K16 |
| Burnaby Way BT12 | | |
| *off Burnaby Pl* | 19 | K16 |
| Burntollet Way BT6 | 27 | R21 |
| Burren Way BT6 | 27 | R20 |
| Bute St BT15 | 14 | N11 |
| Butler Pl BT14 | 13 | H12 |
| Butler St BT14 | 13 | J12 |
| Butler Wk BT14 | 13 | H12 |
| Buttermilk Loney BT14 | 13 | G8 |
| Byron Pl Ms, Hol. BT18 | 11 | Z6 |

## C

| Street | Pg | Grid |
|---|---|---|
| Cabin Hill Ct BT4 | 23 | Y16 |
| Cabin Hill Gdns BT5 | 23 | Y17 |
| Cabin Hill Ms BT5 | 23 | Y16 |
| Cabin Hill Pk BT5 | 22 | X17 |
| Cable Cl BT4 | | |
| *off Newtownards Rd* | 21 | R15 |
| Cadogan Pk BT9 | 25 | J20 |
| Cadogan St BT7 | 26 | N19 |
| Cairnburn Av BT4 | 22 | X13 |
| Cairnburn Cres BT4 | 22 | X13 |
| Cairnburn Dell BT4 | | |
| *off Cairnburn Cres* | 22 | X13 |
| Cairnburn Dr BT4 | 22 | X13 |
| Cairnburn Gdns BT4 | 22 | X13 |
| Cairnburn Gra BT4 | 22 | X13 |
| Cairnburn Pk BT4 | 22 | X13 |
| Cairnburn Rd BT4 | 22 | X14 |
| Cairndale BT13 | 13 | F11 |
| Cairnmartin Rd BT13 | 19 | G13 |
| Cairns, The BT4 | 22 | W15 |
| Cairns St BT12 | 19 | J16 |
| Cairo St BT7 | 26 | N19 |
| Caledon Ct BT13 | 19 | H14 |
| Caledon St BT13 | 19 | H14 |
| California St BT13 | | |
| *off North Boundary St* | 20 | L14 |
| Callan Way BT6 | 27 | R21 |
| Callender St BT1 | 30 | D2 |
| Calvin St BT5 | 21 | R16 |
| Camberwell Ct BT15 | | |
| *off Limestone Rd* | 14 | L11 |
| Camberwell Ter BT15 | 14 | L11 |
| Cambourne Pk BT9 | 25 | H24 |
| Cambrai Cotts BT13 | 19 | J13 |
| Cambrai Ct BT13 | 19 | H14 |
| Cambrai St BT13 | 19 | H13 |
| Cambridge St BT15 | | |
| *off Canning St* | 14 | N12 |
| Camden St BT9 | 20 | L18 |
| Cameronian Dr BT5 | 28 | T19 |
| Cameron St BT7 | 20 | M18 |
| Camlough Pl BT6 | 28 | U20 |
| Campbell Chase BT4 | 23 | Y15 |
| Campbell Ct BT4 | 22 | W15 |
| Campbell Pk Av BT4 | 22 | W15 |
| Canada St BT6 | 21 | Q17 |
| Candahar St BT7 | 26 | N20 |
| Canmore Cl BT13 | 19 | J15 |
| Canmore Ct BT13 | | |
| *off Canmore St* | 19 | J15 |
| Canmore St BT13 | 19 | J15 |
| Canning Pl BT15 | | |
| *off Canning St* | 14 | N12 |
| Canning's Ct BT13 | | |
| *off Shankill Rd* | 19 | K14 |
| Canning St BT15 | 14 | N12 |
| Canterbury St BT7 | 20 | N18 |
| Canton Ct BT6 | | |
| *off Willowfield St* | 21 | R17 |
| Cappagh Gdns BT6 | | |
| *off South Bk* | 27 | R21 |
| Cappy St BT6 | 21 | Q17 |
| Capstone St BT9 | 25 | H21 |
| Cardigan Dr BT14 | 14 | K10 |
| Carew St BT4 | 21 | S15 |
| Cargill St BT13 | 20 | L14 |
| Carlingford St BT6 | 21 | R18 |
| Carlisle Circ BT14 | 20 | L13 |
| Carlisle Par BT15 | 20 | M13 |
| Carlisle Rd BT15 | 20 | M13 |
| Carlisle Sq BT15 | | |
| *off Carlisle Ter* | 20 | M13 |
| Carlisle Ter BT15 | 20 | M13 |

**35**

| Street | Pg | Ref |
|---|---|---|
| Connsbrook Pk BT4 | 21 | T14 |
| Connswater Gro BT4 | 21 | S15 |
| Connswater Link BT5 | 21 | S16 |
| Connswater Ms BT4 | 21 | S15 |
| Connswater Shop Cen BT5 | | |
| *off Bloomfield Av* | 21 | S16 |
| Connswater St BT4 | 21 | S15 |
| Conor Cl BT11 | 24 | C21 |
| Conor Ri BT11 | 24 | C21 |
| Constance St BT5 | 21 | R16 |
| Convention Ct BT4 | 21 | R15 |
| Convention Wk BT4 | | |
| *off Newtownards Rd* | 21 | R15 |
| Conway Ct BT13 | | |
| *off Conway St* | 19 | J14 |
| Conway Link BT13 | 19 | J15 |
| Conway Sq BT13 | | |
| *off Conway Link* | 19 | K15 |
| Conway St BT13 | 19 | J15 |
| Conway Wk BT13 | 19 | K14 |
| Cooke Ct BT7 | 31 | F6 |
| Cooke Ms BT7 | 20 | N18 |
| Cooke Pl BT7 | | |
| *off Cooke Ms* | 20 | N18 |
| Cooke St BT7 | 20 | N18 |
| Cooldarragh Pk BT14 | 8 | K8 |
| Cooldarragh Pk N BT14 | 8 | K8 |
| Coolfin St BT12 | 19 | K18 |
| Coolmore St BT12 | 19 | K18 |
| Coolmoyne Pk BT15 | 8 | L7 |
| Coolnasilla Av BT11 | 24 | D19 |
| Coolnasilla Cl BT11 | 24 | D19 |
| Coolnasilla Dr BT11 | 24 | D19 |
| Coolnasilla Gdns BT11 | 24 | D19 |
| Coolnasilla Pk BT11 | 24 | D19 |
| Coolnasilla Pk E BT11 | 24 | D20 |
| Coolnasilla Pk S BT11 | 24 | D20 |
| Coolnasilla Pk W BT11 | 24 | D20 |
| Coombehill Pk BT14 | 8 | H8 |
| Cooneen Way BT6 | 27 | R20 |
| Corby Way BT11 | 24 | D20 |
| Cormorant Pk BT5 | 28 | W20 |
| Corn Mkt BT1 | 31 | E2 |
| Coronation Ct BT15 | | |
| *off Little York St* | 20 | N14 |
| Corporation Sq BT1 | 20 | N14 |
| Corporation St BT1 | 20 | N14 |
| Corrib Av BT11 | 24 | B21 |
| Corry Link BT3 | 20 | P13 |
| Corry Pl BT3 | 20 | P13 |
| Corry Rd BT3 | 20 | P13 |
| Cosgrave Ct BT15 | | |
| *off Mervue St* | 14 | M12 |
| Cosgrave Hts BT15 | 14 | M12 |
| Cosgrave St BT15 | 14 | N12 |
| Courtrai St BT13 | | |
| *off Mill St W* | 19 | J13 |
| Court St BT13 | 20 | L13 |
| Coyle's Pl BT7 | | |
| *off Coyle St* | 31 | E6 |
| Coyle St BT7 | 31 | E6 |
| Craigmore Way BT7 | | |
| *off Apsley St* | 30 | D5 |
| Craigs Ter BT13 | 19 | K14 |
| *off Dundee St* | | |
| Craigtara, Hol. BT18 | 11 | Z7 |
| Cranbrook Ct BT14 | 13 | H11 |
| Cranbrook Gdns BT14 | 13 | H11 |
| Cranburn Pl BT14 | | |
| *off Lincoln Av* | 20 | L13 |
| Cranburn St BT14 | 20 | L13 |
| Cranmore Av BT9 | 25 | J21 |
| Cranmore Gdns BT9 | 25 | J21 |
| Cranmore Pk BT9 | 25 | J21 |
| Cranton Ct BT6 | 21 | R17 |
| Craven St BT7 | | |
| *off Rumford St* | 19 | K14 |
| Crawford Pk BT6 | 28 | V21 |
| Creeslough Gdns BT11 | 24 | B21 |
| Creeve Wk BT11 | 24 | E20 |
| Creevy Av BT5 | 29 | X20 |
| Creevy Way BT5 | 29 | X19 |
| Cregagh Ct BT6 | | |
| *off Cregagh Rd* | 27 | S19 |
| Cregagh Pk BT6 | 27 | S21 |
| Cregagh Pk E BT6 | 27 | S21 |
| Cregagh Rd BT6 | 21 | R18 |
| Cregagh St BT6 | 21 | R18 |
| Crescent, The BT7 | 26 | N22 |
| Crescent, The, Hol. BT18 | 11 | AA5 |
| Crescent Gdns BT7 | 20 | M18 |
| Crescent La BT7 | | |
| *off Lower Cres* | 20 | M18 |
| Cricklewood Cres BT9 | 26 | M22 |
| Cricklewood Pk BT9 | 26 | M22 |
| Crimea Cl BT13 | 19 | K14 |
| Crimea Ct BT13 | 19 | K14 |
| Crimea St BT13 | 19 | K14 |
| Croaghan Gdns BT11 | | |
| *off South Grn* | 24 | E20 |
| Crocus St BT12 | 19 | J16 |
| Croft Gdns, Hol. BT18 | 11 | BB5 |
| Crofthouse Ct BT5 | | |
| *off Kilmory Gdns* | 23 | AA18 |
| Croft Manor, Hol. BT18 | 11 | BB6 |
| Croft Meadows, Hol. BT18 | 11 | BB5 |
| Crofton Glen, Hol. BT18 | 11 | BB5 |
| Croft Rd, Hol. BT18 | 11 | BB5 |
| Cromac Av BT7 | 31 | E5 |
| Cromac Pl BT7 | 31 | F6 |
| Cromac Quay BT7 | 31 | F6 |
| Cromac Sq BT2 | 31 | F4 |
| Cromac St BT2 | 31 | E5 |
| Cromwell Rd BT7 | 20 | M18 |
| Crosby St BT13 | | |
| *off Percy Pl* | 20 | L14 |
| Crosscollyer St BT15 | 14 | M12 |
| Crossland Ct BT13 | 19 | J15 |
| Crossland St BT13 | | |
| *off Canmore St* | 19 | J14 |
| Cross Par BT7 | 27 | P20 |
| Crown Entry BT1 | | |
| *off High St* | 31 | E2 |
| Crumlin Gdns BT13 | 13 | H12 |
| Crumlin Rd BT14 | 12 | E7 |
| Crystal St BT5 | 21 | T16 |
| Cuan Par BT13 | 19 | H14 |
| Cuba Wk BT4 | 21 | R15 |
| Cullingtree Rd BT12 | 19 | K16 |
| Culmore Gdns BT11 | 24 | B20 |
| Cultra St BT15 | 14 | N12 |
| Cumberland St BT13 | 19 | K14 |
| Cumberland Wk BT13 | | |
| *off Percy St* | 19 | K14 |
| Cupar St BT13 | 19 | H15 |
| Cupar St Lwr BT13 | 19 | J15 |
| Cupar Way BT13 | 19 | J15 |
| Curtis St BT1 | 20 | M14 |
| Curzon St BT7 | 26 | N19 |
| Cussick St BT9 | 26 | K19 |
| Custom Ho Sq BT1 | 31 | F1 |
| Cutters La BT9 | 26 | M22 |
| Cyprus Av BT5 | 22 | U16 |
| Cyprus Gdns BT5 | 22 | U16 |
| Cyprus Pk BT5 | 22 | U16 |
| **D** | | |
| Dairy St BT12 | | |
| *off Shiels St* | 19 | H17 |
| Daisyfield St BT13 | 19 | K13 |
| Daisyhill Ct BT12 | | |
| *off Westrock Gdns* | 19 | G16 |
| Dalebrook Av BT11 | 24 | C22 |
| Dalebrook Pk BT11 | 24 | C22 |
| Dalry Pk BT5 | 23 | AA17 |
| Dalton St BT5 | 31 | H1 |
| Damascus St BT7 | 20 | N18 |
| Dandy St, New. BT36 | 9 | N4 |
| Danesfort BT9 | 26 | K21 |
| Danesfort Pk Cl BT9 | 26 | L22 |
| Danesfort Pk Dr BT9 | 26 | L22 |
| Danesfort Pk Mt BT9 | 26 | L22 |
| Danesfort Pk Pl BT9 | 26 | L22 |
| Danesfort Pk S BT9 | 26 | L22 |
| Danesfort Pk W BT9 | 26 | L22 |
| Danesfort Pk Wd BT9 | 26 | L22 |
| Danns Row BT6 | | |
| *off Ravenhill Rd* | 21 | Q16 |
| Danube St BT13 | 19 | J13 |
| Daphne St BT12 | 19 | K18 |
| Dargan Br BT1 | 31 | G1 |
| Dargan Br BT3 | 31 | G1 |
| Dargan Cres BT3 | 15 | P9 |
| Dargan Dr BT3 | 15 | R9 |
| Dargan Rd BT3 | 9 | P8 |
| Dart Hill BT11 | 24 | E21 |
| David St BT13 | 21 | J15 |
| Dawson St BT15 | 20 | M13 |
| Dayton St BT13 | 20 | L14 |
| Deacon St BT15 | 14 | N11 |
| Deanby Gdns BT14 | 13 | J10 |
| Dean Crooks Fold BT5 | 22 | U16 |
| Deerpark Ct BT14 | 13 | J11 |
| Deerpark Dr BT14 | 13 | H10 |
| Deerpark Gdns BT14 | 13 | H10 |
| Deerpark Gro BT14 | 13 | J11 |
| Deerpark Ms BT14 | 13 | J11 |
| Deerpark Par BT14 | 13 | H10 |
| Deerpark Rd BT14 | 13 | H10 |
| Dee St BT4 | 21 | S15 |
| Dehra Gro BT4 | 22 | U15 |
| Delamont Pk BT6 | 28 | U21 |
| Delaware St BT6 | 21 | Q17 |
| Delhi Par BT7 | 26 | N19 |
| Delhi St BT7 | 26 | N19 |
| Demesne Av, Hol. BT18 | 11 | AA7 |
| Demesne Cl, Hol. BT18 | 11 | AA7 |
| Demesne Gro, Hol. BT18 | 11 | AA7 |
| Demesne Manor, Hol. BT18 | 11 | AA6 |
| Demesne Pk, Hol. BT18 | 11 | AA7 |
| Demesne Rd, Hol. BT18 | 11 | Z8 |
| Denewood Dr BT11 | 24 | E19 |
| Denewood Pk BT11 | 24 | E19 |
| Denmark St BT13 | 20 | L14 |
| Dennet End BT6 | 27 | R20 |
| Denorrton Pk BT4 | 22 | U14 |
| Depot Rd BT3 | 16 | W11 |
| Deramore Av BT7 | 26 | N21 |
| Deramore Ct BT9 | | |
| *off Deramore Pk S* | 26 | L23 |
| Deramore Dr BT9 | 26 | K23 |
| Deramore Gdns BT7 | 26 | N21 |
| Deramore Pk BT9 | 26 | K23 |
| Deramore Pk S BT9 | 26 | K23 |
| Deramore St BT7 | 27 | P20 |
| Derby Ter BT12 | | |
| *off Divis St* | 19 | K15 |
| Derlett St BT7 | 26 | N20 |
| Dermott Hill Dr BT12 | 18 | D16 |
| Dermott Hill Gdns BT12 | 18 | D16 |
| Dermott Hill Grn BT12 | 18 | D16 |
| Dermott Hill Gro BT12 | 18 | D16 |
| Dermott Hill Par BT12 | 18 | D16 |
| Dermott Hill Pk BT12 | 18 | D16 |
| Dermott Hill Rd BT12 | 18 | D16 |
| Dermott Hill Way BT12 | 18 | D16 |
| Derrin Pas BT12 | 24 | E20 |
| Derryvolgie Av BT9 | 26 | K20 |
| Derryvolgie Ms BT9 | 26 | K20 |
| Derwent St BT4 | 21 | R15 |
| Devenish Ct BT13 | | |
| *off Cupar St Lwr* | 19 | J15 |
| Devon Dr BT4 | 21 | T14 |
| Devon Par BT4 | 21 | T14 |
| Devonshire Cl BT12 | 30 | A3 |
| Devonshire Pl BT12 | 30 | A3 |
| Devonshire St BT12 | 30 | A3 |
| Devonshire Way BT12 | 30 | A3 |
| Dewey St BT13 | 19 | J14 |
| Dhu-Varren Cres BT13 | 19 | H14 |
| Dhu-Varren Par BT13 | 19 | H14 |
| Dhu-Varren St BT13 | 19 | H14 |
| Diamond Av BT10 | 24 | E23 |
| Diamond Gdns BT10 | 24 | E23 |
| Diamond Gro BT10 | 24 | E23 |
| Diamond St BT13 | | |
| *off Dover Pl* | 20 | L14 |
| Dill Rd BT6 | 27 | S20 |
| Disraeli Cl BT13 | 19 | H13 |
| Disraeli Ct BT13 | 19 | H12 |
| Disraeli St BT13 | 19 | H13 |
| Disraeli Wk BT13 | | |
| *off Disraeli St* | 13 | H12 |
| Distillery Ct BT12 | | |
| *off Distillery St* | 19 | K16 |
| Distillery St BT12 | 19 | K16 |
| Distillery Way BT12 | | |
| *off Distillery St* | 19 | K17 |
| Divis Ct BT12 | 30 | A2 |
| Divis Dr BT11 | 18 | F18 |
| Divismore Cres BT12 | 18 | E16 |
| Divismore Pk BT12 | 18 | F16 |
| Divismore Way BT12 | 18 | E16 |
| Divis St BT12 | 19 | K15 |
| Dock La BT15 | | |
| *off Dock St* | 20 | N13 |
| Dock St BT15 | 20 | N13 |
| Dock St Ms BT15 | | |
| *off Dock St* | 20 | N13 |
| Donaldson Cres BT13 | 13 | G12 |
| Donard St BT6 | 21 | Q17 |
| Donegall Arc BT1 | 30 | D2 |
| Donegall Av BT12 | 25 | J19 |
| Donegall Gdns BT12 | 25 | J19 |
| Donegall La BT1 | 20 | M14 |
| Donegall Par BT12 | 19 | J18 |
| Donegall Pk BT10 | 25 | F23 |
| Donegall Pk Av BT15 | 8 | L6 |
| Donegall Pass BT7 | 30 | C6 |
| Donegall Pl BT1 | 30 | D2 |
| Donegall Quay BT1 | 20 | N14 |
| Donegall Rd BT12 | 19 | G17 |
| Donegall Sq E BT1 | 30 | D3 |
| Donegall Sq Ms BT2 | 30 | D3 |
| Donegall Sq N BT1 | 30 | D3 |
| Donegall Sq S BT1 | 30 | D3 |
| Donegall Sq W BT1 | 30 | D3 |
| Donegall St BT1 | 30 | D3 |
| Donegall St Pl BT1 | | |
| *off Donegall St* | 30 | D1 |
| Donegore Gdns BT11 | 24 | B23 |
| Donnybrook St BT9 | 26 | K19 |
| Donore Ct BT15 | | |
| *off New Lo Rd* | 14 | M12 |
| Donore Pl BT15 | | |
| *off Stratheden St* | 14 | M12 |
| Donovan Ct BT6 | 27 | S19 |
| Donovan Par BT6 | 27 | S19 |
| Doon Cotts BT11 | 24 | B22 |
| Doon End BT10 | 25 | F24 |
| Doon Rd BT11 | 24 | B22 |
| Dorchester Pk BT9 | 25 | J24 |
| Douglas Ct BT4 | | |
| *off Dundela Av* | 22 | U15 |
| Dover Ct BT13 | | |
| *off Dover St* | 20 | L14 |
| Dover Pl BT13 | 20 | L14 |
| Dover St BT13 | 20 | L14 |
| Dover Wk BT13 | | |
| *off Dover St* | 20 | L14 |
| Downfine Gdns BT11 | 18 | D18 |
| Downfine Wk BT11 | 18 | E18 |
| Downing St BT13 | 19 | K14 |
| Downpatrick St BT4 | 21 | S15 |
| Downshire Ms, Hol. BT18 | 11 | Z6 |
| Downshire Par BT6 | | |
| *off Hamel Dr* | 27 | S21 |
| Downshire Pk Cen BT6 | 27 | S21 |
| Downshire Pk E BT6 | 27 | S20 |
| Downshire Pk N BT6 | 27 | S21 |
| Downshire Pk S BT6 | 27 | S21 |
| Downshire Pl BT2 | | |
| *off Great Victoria St* | 30 | C5 |
| Downshire Pl, Hol. BT18 | 11 | Z6 |
| Downshire Rd BT6 | 27 | R22 |
| Downshire Rd, Hol. BT18 | 11 | Z6 |
| Downview Av BT15 | 9 | M6 |
| Downview Cres BT15 | 9 | M6 |
| Downview Dr BT15 | 9 | M6 |
| Downview Gdns BT15 | 9 | N6 |
| Downview Lo BT15 | 9 | M5 |
| Downview Manor BT15 | 9 | N6 |
| Downview Ms BT15 | 9 | N6 |
| Downview Pk BT15 | 9 | M6 |
| Downview Pk W BT15 | 8 | L7 |
| Drenia BT11 | 24 | C23 |
| Drinagh Manor BT5 | 22 | X18 |
| Drive, The BT9 | 26 | L22 |
| Dromara St BT7 | 26 | N19 |
| Dromore St BT7 | 21 | R19 |
| Drumkeen Ct BT8 | 27 | Q23 |

|  | | |
|---|---|---|
| Drumkeen Manor BT8 | | |
| *off Saintfield Rd* | 27 | Q23 |
| Drummond Pk BT9 | 25 | H24 |
| Drumragh End BT6 | 27 | R21 |
| Dublin Rd BT2 | 30 | C6 |
| Dublin St BT6 | 21 | Q17 |
| Dudley St BT7 | 20 | N18 |
| Dufferin Rd BT3 | 15 | P12 |
| Duffield Pk BT13 | 18 | F13 |
| Duke St BT5 | | |
| *off Susan St* | 21 | Q15 |
| Dunbar Link BT12 | 20 | N14 |
| Dunbar St BT1 | 20 | N14 |
| Dunblane Av BT14 | 13 | J10 |
| Dunboyne Pk BT13 | 18 | F15 |
| Duncairn Av BT14 | 14 | L12 |
| Duncairn Gdns BT15 | 14 | M12 |
| Duncairn Par BT15 | 20 | M13 |
| Duncoole Pk BT14 | 8 | J7 |
| Duncrue Cres BT3 | 15 | P9 |
| Duncrue Link BT3 | 15 | P9 |
| Duncrue Pass BT3 | 15 | P10 |
| Duncrue Pl BT3 | 15 | P10 |
| Duncrue Rd BT3 | 15 | P10 |
| Duncrue St BT3 | 15 | P10 |
| Dundee St BT13 | 19 | K14 |
| Dundela Av BT4 | 22 | U15 |
| Dundela Cl BT4 | | |
| *off Wilgar St* | 22 | U15 |
| Dundela Ct BT4 | · | |
| *off Dundela St* | 22 | U15 |
| Dundela Cres BT4 | 22 | U15 |
| Dundela Dr BT4 | 22 | U15 |
| Dundela Flats BT4 | 22 | U15 |
| Dundela Gdns BT4 | 22 | U15 |
| Dundela Pk BT4 | 21 | T15 |
| Dundela St BT4 | 22 | U15 |
| Dundela Vw BT4 | | |
| *off Dundela Av* | 22 | U15 |
| Duneden Pk BT14 | 13 | H12 |
| Dunkeld Gdns BT14 | 13 | J10 |
| Dunlambert Av BT15 | 14 | M9 |
| Dunlambert Dr BT15 | 14 | M9 |
| Dunlambert Gdns BT15 | 14 | N9 |
| Dunlambert Pk BT15 | 14 | M9 |
| Dunlewey St BT13 | 19 | J15 |
| Dunlewey Wk BT13 | | |
| *off Dunlewey St* | 19 | J16 |
| Dunluce Av BT9 | 19 | K18 |
| Dunmisk Pk BT11 | 24 | E20 |
| Dunmisk Ter BT11 | | |
| *off Commedagh Dr* | 24 | E20 |
| Dunmore Av BT15 | 14 | M10 |
| Dunmore Ct BT15 | 14 | M10 |
| Dunmore Cres BT15 | 14 | L10 |
| Dunmore Dr BT15 | 14 | L10 |
| Dunmore Ms BT15 | 14 | M10 |
| Dunmore Pk BT15 | 14 | M10 |
| Dunmore Pl BT15 | 14 | M10 |
| Dunmore St BT13 | 19 | J15 |
| Dunmoyle St BT13 | 19 | H14 |
| Dunmurry Lo BT10 | 24 | C24 |
| Dunowen Gdns BT14 | 13 | J10 |
| Dunraven Av BT5 | 21 | T17 |
| Dunraven Ct BT5 | 21 | T17 |
| Dunraven Cres BT5 | 21 | T17 |
| Dunraven Dr BT5 | 21 | T17 |
| Dunraven Gdns BT5 | 21 | T17 |
| Dunraven Par BT5 | 21 | T17 |
| Dunraven Pk BT5 | 21 | T17 |
| Dunraven St BT13 | | |
| *off Rumford St* | 19 | K14 |
| Dunvegan St BT6 | 21 | Q17 |
| Dunville St BT12 | 19 | J16 |
| Durham Ct BT12 | 30 | A2 |
| Durham St BT12 | 30 | B2 |
| **E** | | |
| Ean Hill, Hol. BT18 | 11 | Z6 |
| Earl Cl BT15 | 20 | M13 |
| Earl Haig Cres BT6 | 21 | R18 |
| Earl Haig Par BT6 | 27 | R19 |
| Earl Haig Pk BT6 | 27 | R19 |
| Earls Ct, The BT4 | | |
| *off Bethany St* | 22 | V16 |
| Earlscourt St BT12 | 19 | J16 |
| Earlswood Ct BT4 | | |
| *off Kincora Av* | 22 | W16 |
| Earlswood Gro BT4 | 22 | W15 |
| Earlswood Pk BT4 | 22 | V15 |
| Earlswood Rd BT4 | 22 | V15 |
| East Bread St BT5 | 21 | S16 |
| East Br St BT1 | 31 | F3 |
| Eastleigh Cres BT5 | 22 | V16 |
| Eastleigh Dale BT4 | 22 | W16 |
| Eastleigh Dr BT4 | 22 | V16 |
| East Link, Hol. BT18 | 11 | Z8 |
| Easton Av BT14 | 14 | K11 |
| Easton Cres BT14 | 14 | K11 |
| East Twin Rd BT3 | 15 | S11 |
| Eblana St BT7 | 20 | M18 |
| Ebor Dr BT12 | 25 | J19 |
| Ebor Par BT12 | 25 | J19 |
| Ebor St BT12 | 25 | J19 |
| Ebrington Gdns BT4 | 22 | U16 |
| Eccles St BT13 | 19 | J14 |
| Edenbrook Cl BT13 | 19 | J13 |
| Eden Ct BT4 | 22 | V15 |
| Edenderry Cl BT13 | 19 | J13 |
| Edenderry St BT13 | 19 | J13 |
| Edenmore Dr BT11 | 24 | C21 |
| Edenvale Cres BT4 | 22 | V15 |
| Edenvale Dr BT4 | 22 | V15 |
| Edenvale Gdns BT4 | 22 | V15 |
| Edenvale Gro BT4 | 22 | V15 |
| Edenvale Pk BT4 | 22 | V15 |
| Edgar St BT5 | 21 | Q16 |
| Edgecumbe Dr BT4 | 22 | V15 |
| Edgecumbe Gdns BT4 | 22 | V14 |
| Edgecumbe Pk BT4 | 22 | V14 |
| Edgecumbe Vw BT4 | 22 | V14 |
| Edgewater Dr BT3 | 15 | S8 |
| Edgewater Rd BT3 | 15 | R8 |
| Edinburgh Av, Hol. | | |
| BT18 | 11 | BB7 |
| Edinburgh Ms BT9 | 26 | K19 |
| Edinburgh St BT9 | 25 | J19 |
| Edith St BT5 | 21 | R16 |
| Edlingham St BT15 | 14 | M12 |
| Edwina St BT13 | | |
| *off Riga St* | 19 | J14 |
| Egeria St BT12 | 19 | K18 |
| Eglantine Av BT9 | 26 | K19 |
| Eglantine Gdns BT9 | 26 | L19 |
| Eglantine Pl BT9 | 26 | K19 |
| Egmont Gdns BT12 | 30 | A6 |
| Eia St BT14 | 14 | L12 |
| Eileen Gdns BT9 | 26 | K20 |
| Elaine St BT9 | 26 | M19 |
| Elesington Ct BT6 | | |
| *off Mayfair Av* | 27 | S20 |
| Elgin St BT7 | 26 | N19 |
| Elimgrove St BT14 | 14 | K11 |
| Elizabeth Rd, Hol. | | |
| BT18 | 11 | BB6 |
| Eliza Pl BT7 | | |
| *off Eliza St* | 31 | F4 |
| Eliza St BT7 | 31 | F4 |
| Eliza St Cl BT7 | 31 | F4 |
| Eliza St Ter BT7 | 31 | F5 |
| Elm Ct BT7 | 30 | D6 |
| Elmdale St BT5 | 21 | T16 |
| Elmfield St BT14 | 14 | K11 |
| Elmgrove Manor BT5 | 21 | S17 |
| Elmgrove Rd BT5 | 21 | S17 |
| Elm St BT7 | 30 | D6 |
| Elmwood Av BT9 | 20 | L18 |
| Elmwood Ms BT9 | 20 | L18 |
| Elsmere Hts BT5 | 29 | AA19 |
| Elsmere Manor BT5 | 29 | AA19 |
| Elsmere Pk BT5 | 29 | AA19 |
| Elswick St BT12 | 19 | H15 |
| Emerald St BT6 | 21 | Q15 |
| Empire Dr BT12 | 19 | K17 |
| Empire Par BT12 | 19 | K17 |
| Empire St BT12 | 19 | J17 |
| Enfield Dr BT13 | 19 | H13 |
| Enfield Par BT13 | 19 | H13 |
| Enfield St BT13 | 19 | H13 |
| Enid Dr BT5 | 22 | V16 |
| Enid Par BT5 | 22 | V16 |
| Epworth St BT5 | 21 | R16 |
| Erin Way BT7 | 30 | D5 |
| Errigal Pk BT11 | 24 | D21 |
| Erris Gro BT11 | | |
| *off Oranmore Dr* | 24 | B23 |
| Erskine St BT5 | 21 | R16 |
| Eskdale Gdns BT14 | 13 | H11 |
| Esmond St BT13 | 19 | J14 |
| *off Shankill Rd* | 19 | J14 |
| Espie Way BT6 | 28 | U20 |
| Esplanade, The, Hol. | | |
| BT18 | 11 | Y6 |
| Essex Gro BT7 | 20 | N18 |
| Esther St BT15 | 14 | N11 |
| Estoril Ct BT14 | 13 | H12 |
| Estoril Pk BT14 | 13 | H12 |
| Ethel St BT9 | 25 | J20 |
| Etna Dr BT14 | 13 | H11 |
| Eureka St BT12 | 30 | A6 |
| Euston Par BT6 | 21 | R18 |
| Euston St BT6 | 21 | R17 |
| Euterpe St BT12 | 19 | K18 |
| Evelyn Av BT5 | 21 | T16 |
| Evelyn Gdns BT15 | 14 | L9 |
| Eversleigh St BT6 | 21 | Q17 |
| Everton Dr BT6 | 27 | S22 |
| Evewilliam Pk BT15 | 14 | L9 |
| Evolina St BT15 | 14 | M12 |
| Exchange Pl BT1 | | |
| *off Donegall St* | 31 | E1 |
| Exchange St W BT1 | 20 | N14 |
| Excise Wk BT12 | 19 | K16 |
| **F** | | |
| Faburn Pk BT14 | 13 | G10 |
| Factory St BT5 | | |
| *off East Bread St* | 21 | S16 |
| Fairfax Ct BT14 | 14 | K12 |
| Fairhill Gdns BT15 | 9 | M7 |
| Fairhill Pk BT15 | 9 | M7 |
| Fairhill Wk BT15 | 9 | M7 |
| Fairhill Way BT15 | 9 | M7 |
| Fairway Gdns BT5 | 29 | X20 |
| Falcon Rd BT12 | 25 | J20 |
| Falcon Way BT12 | | |
| *off Falcon Rd* | 25 | J20 |
| Falls Ct BT13 | | |
| *off Conway Link* | 19 | J15 |
| Falls Rd BT11 | 25 | F19 |
| Falls Rd BT12 | 18 | F18 |
| Fallswater Dr BT12 | | |
| *off Falls Rd* | 19 | H17 |
| Fallswater St BT12 | 19 | H17 |
| Fane St BT9 | 19 | K18 |
| Farmhill Rd, Hol. BT18 | 11 | BB4 |
| Farmhurst Grn BT5 | 29 | Y19 |
| Farmhurst Way BT5 | 29 | Y19 |
| Farnham St BT7 | 20 | N18 |
| Farringdon Ct BT14 | 13 | H11 |
| Farringdon Gdns BT14 | 13 | H11 |
| Fashoda St BT5 | 21 | S17 |
| Federation St BT6 | 21 | Q18 |
| Felt St BT12 | 30 | A6 |
| Ferguson Dr BT4 | 22 | U15 |
| Ferndale St BT9 | | |
| *off Lisburn Rd* | 25 | J20 |
| Fernhill Gro BT13 | 13 | F11 |
| Fernhill Hts BT13 | 13 | F12 |
| Fern St BT12 | | |
| *off Frome St* | 21 | R15 |
| Fernvale St BT14 | 22 | U14 |
| Fernwood St BT7 | 26 | N20 |
| Fife St BT14 | 14 | N11 |
| Fifth St BT13 | 19 | K15 |
| Finaghy Pk Cen BT10 | 24 | D24 |
| Finaghy Pk N BT10 | 24 | E23 |
| Finaghy Pk S BT10 | 24 | E24 |
| Finaghy Rd N BT10 | 24 | E23 |
| Finaghy Rd N BT11 | 24 | D21 |
| Finaghy Rd S BT10 | 24 | E24 |
| Finbank Ct BT9 | 25 | G24 |
| Finbank Gdns BT9 | 25 | G24 |
| Finch Cl BT9 | 25 | H24 |
| Finch Ct BT9 | | |
| *off Finch Way* | 25 | H24 |
| Finch Gro BT9 | 25 | H24 |
| Finchley Dr BT4 | 22 | X13 |
| Finchley Gdns BT4 | | |
| *off Finchley Pk* | 22 | X13 |
| Finchley Pk BT4 | 22 | X13 |
| Finchley Vale BT4 | 22 | X13 |
| Finch Pl BT9 | | |
| *off Finch Gro* | 25 | H24 |
| Finch Way BT9 | 25 | H24 |
| Findon Gdns BT9 | 25 | G24 |
| Findon Gro BT9 | 25 | H24 |
| Findon Pl BT9 | 25 | H24 |
| Fingals Ct BT13 | 30 | A1 |
| Fingal St BT13 | 11 | H13 |
| Finlay Pk, New. BT36 | 9 | N4 |
| Finmore Ct BT4 | 21 | R15 |
| Finnis Cl BT9 | 25 | G24 |
| Finnis Dr BT9 | 25 | G24 |
| Finn Sq BT13 | 30 | A1 |
| Finsbury St BT6 | 27 | R19 |
| Finvoy St BT5 | 21 | T16 |
| Finwood Ct BT9 | 25 | G24 |
| Finwood Pk BT9 | 25 | G24 |
| Firmount BT15 | 14 | L9 |
| Firmount Ct, Hol. | | |
| BT18 | 17 | Z9 |
| Firmount Cres, Hol. | | |
| BT18 | 17 | Z9 |
| First St BT13 | 19 | K15 |
| Fisherwick Pl BT1 | | |
| *off College Sq E* | 30 | C3 |
| Fitzroy Av BT7 | 20 | M18 |
| Fitzroy Ct BT7 | | |
| *off Fitzroy Av* | 20 | M18 |
| Fitzwilliam Av BT7 | 27 | P21 |
| Fitzwilliam Sq BT7 | 20 | N18 |
| Fitzwilliam St BT9 | 20 | L18 |
| Flaxcentre BT14 | 13 | J12 |
| Flax St BT14 | 13 | J12 |
| Flaxton Pl BT14 | | |
| *off Old Mill Rd* | 12 | E9 |
| Fleetwood St BT14 | | |
| *off Crumlin Rd* | 20 | L13 |
| Flora St BT5 | 21 | S17 |
| Flora St Walkway BT5 | 21 | S17 |
| Florence Ct BT13 | 20 | L13 |
| Florence Pl BT13 | 20 | L13 |
| Florence Sq BT13 | 20 | L13 |
| Florenceville Av BT7 | 27 | P21 |
| Florenceville Dr BT7 | 27 | P21 |
| Florence Wk BT13 | | |
| *off Hopewell Av* | 20 | L13 |
| Florida Dr BT6 | 21 | Q18 |
| Florida St BT6 | 21 | Q17 |
| Flush Dr BT6 | 27 | Q21 |
| Flush Gdns BT6 | 27 | Q21 |
| Flush Grn BT6 | 27 | Q21 |
| Flush Pk BT6 | 27 | Q21 |
| Flush Rd BT14 | 12 | D7 |
| Fodnamona Ct BT11 | | |
| *off Aitnamona Cres* | 24 | D19 |
| Forest Hill BT9 | 26 | K23 |
| Forest St BT12 | 19 | H15 |
| Forfar La BT12 | 19 | H15 |
| Forfar St BT12 | 19 | H15 |
| Forfar Way BT12 | 19 | H15 |
| Formby Pk BT14 | 13 | H9 |
| Forster St BT13 | | |
| *off Ariel St* | 19 | K14 |
| Forsythe St BT13 | | |
| *off Dover Pl* | 20 | L14 |
| Fortfield Pl BT15 | 14 | M12 |
| Forthbrook Ct BT13 | | |
| *off Ballygomartin Rd* | 18 | F13 |
| Forth Par BT13 | 19 | H14 |
| Forthriver Cl BT13 | 12 | E11 |
| Forthriver Cotts BT14 | | |
| *off Ballysillan Rd* | 8 | J8 |
| Forthriver Cres BT13 | 13 | F11 |
| Forthriver Dale BT13 | 12 | E11 |
| Forthriver Dr BT13 | 13 | F11 |
| Forthriver Grn BT13 | 13 | F11 |
| Forthriver Link BT13 | 13 | F11 |
| Forthriver Par BT13 | 12 | E11 |
| Forthriver Pk BT13 | 12 | E10 |
| Forthriver Pas BT13 | 18 | F13 |
| Forthriver Rd BT13 | 12 | E11 |
| Forthriver Way BT13 | 13 | F12 |
| Fort St BT12 | 19 | H15 |
| Fortuna St BT12 | 19 | K18 |
| Fortwilliam | | |
| *off Fortwilliam Pk* | 14 | L9 |
| Fortwilliam Cres BT15 | 14 | N9 |

| Street | No. | Grid |
|---|---|---|
| Fortwilliam Demesne BT15 | 9 | M8 |
| Fortwilliam Dr BT15 | 8 | L8 |
| Fortwilliam Gdns BT15 | 14 | L9 |
| Fortwilliam Gra BT15 | 9 | N8 |
| Fortwilliam Par BT15 | 14 | M9 |
| Fortwilliam Pk BT15 | 14 | L9 |
| Fountain La BT1 | 30 | D2 |
| Fountain St BT1 | 30 | D2 |
| Fountain St N BT15 | | |
| *off New Lo Rd* | 20 | M13 |
| Fountainville Av BT9 | 20 | L18 |
| Four Winds Dr BT8 | 27 | S24 |
| Four Winds Pk BT8 | 27 | S24 |
| Foxglove St BT5 | 21 | S17 |
| Foyle Ct BT14 | 19 | K13 |
| Francis St BT1 | 30 | C1 |
| Franklin St BT2 | 30 | C3 |
| Franklin St Pl BT2 | | |
| *off Franklin St* | 30 | D4 |
| Frank St BT5 | | |
| *off Castlereagh St* | 21 | S16 |
| Frank St BT5 | 21 | R16 |
| Fraser Pass BT4 | | |
| *off Wolff Cl* | 21 | Q15 |
| Fraser St BT3 | 21 | Q14 |
| Frederick La BT1 | | |
| *off Frederick St* | 20 | M14 |
| Frederick Pl BT1 | | |
| *off Frederick St* | 20 | M14 |
| Frederick St BT1 | 20 | M14 |
| Frenchpark St BT12 | 19 | J18 |
| Friendly Pl BT7 | 31 | G4 |
| Friendly Row BT7 | 31 | F4 |
| Friendly St BT7 | 31 | F4 |
| Friendly Way BT7 | 31 | F4 |
| Frome St BT4 | 21 | R15 |
| Fruithill Ct BT11 | 24 | E20 |
| Fruithill Pk BT11 | 24 | E19 |
| Fulton St BT7 | 30 | C6 |

## G

| Street | No. | Grid |
|---|---|---|
| Gaffikin St BT12 | 30 | B6 |
| Gainsborough Dr BT15 | 14 | M11 |
| Galwally Av BT8 | 27 | P23 |
| Galwally Pk BT8 | 27 | Q22 |
| Galway St BT12 | 30 | B2 |
| Gamble St BT1 | 20 | N14 |
| Gardenmore BT15 | | |
| *off Salisbury Av* | 8 | L8 |
| Gardiner Pl BT13 | 20 | L14 |
| Gardiner St BT13 | 30 | B1 |
| Garland Av BT8 | 27 | S24 |
| Garland Cres BT8 | 27 | S24 |
| Garland Grn BT8 | 27 | S24 |
| Garland Hill BT8 | 27 | S24 |
| Garland Pk BT8 | 27 | S24 |
| Garmoyle St BT15 | 20 | N13 |
| Garnerville Dr BT4 | 17 | X12 |
| Garnerville Gdns BT4 | 17 | X12 |
| Garnerville Gro BT4 | 17 | X12 |
| Garnerville Pk BT4 | 17 | X12 |
| Garnerville Rd BT4 | 17 | X12 |
| Garnock BT11 | 24 | C23 |
| Garnock Hill BT10 | 24 | C24 |
| Garnock Hill Pk BT10 | 24 | C24 |
| Garranard Manor BT4 | 22 | W14 |
| Garranard Pk BT4 | 22 | W14 |
| Garron Cres BT10 | 25 | F24 |
| Gartree Pl BT11 | 24 | C20 |
| Gawn St BT4 | 21 | S15 |
| Geary Rd BT5 | 29 | Z19 |
| Geeragh Pl BT10 | 25 | F24 |
| Geneva Gdns BT9 | 26 | M21 |
| Genoa St BT12 | 19 | K16 |
| Geoffrey St BT13 | 19 | J13 |
| Ghent Pl BT13 | | |
| *off Sydney St W* | 19 | J13 |
| Gibson Pk Av BT6 | 27 | S19 |
| Gibson Pk Dr BT6 | | |
| *off Cregagh Rd* | 21 | R18 |
| Gibson Pk Gdns BT6 | 21 | R18 |
| Gibson St BT12 | 19 | K16 |
| Gilbourne Ct BT5 | 29 | Y19 |
| Gilnahirk Av BT5 | 29 | Y19 |
| Gilnahirk Cres BT5 | 29 | Y19 |
| Gilnahirk Dr BT5 | 29 | Y19 |
| Gilnahirk Pk BT5 | 29 | Y19 |

| Street | No. | Grid |
|---|---|---|
| Gilnahirk Ri BT5 | 29 | Y19 |
| Gilnahirk Rd BT5 | 23 | Y17 |
| Gilnahirk Rd W BT5 | 29 | AA20 |
| Gilnahirk Wk BT5 | 29 | Y19 |
| Gipsy St BT7 | 27 | P20 |
| Glandore Av BT15 | 14 | L10 |
| Glandore Dr BT15 | 14 | L10 |
| Glandore Gdns BT15 | 14 | L9 |
| Glandore Par BT15 | | |
| *off Ashfield Gdns* | 14 | M10 |
| Glanleam Dr BT15 | 14 | M10 |
| Glantane Dr BT15 | 14 | L10 |
| Glantrasna Dr BT15 | 14 | M10 |
| Glanworth Dr BT15 | 14 | L10 |
| Glanworth Gdns BT15 | 14 | L10 |
| Glasgow St BT15 | 14 | N11 |
| Glassmullin Gdns BT11 | 24 | D21 |
| Glastonbury Av BT15 | 8 | L7 |
| Glen, The BT15 | 14 | M11 |
| Glenalina Cres BT12 | 18 | E17 |
| Glenalina Gdns BT12 | | |
| *off Glenalina Cres* | 18 | E17 |
| Glenalina Grn BT12 | | |
| *off Glenalina Rd* | 18 | E16 |
| Glenalina Pk BT12 | 18 | E16 |
| Glenalina Pas BT12 | | |
| *off Glenalina Rd* | 18 | E16 |
| Glenalina Rd BT12 | 18 | E16 |
| Glenallen St BT5 | 21 | R16 |
| Glenard Brook BT14 | 14 | K11 |
| Glenbank Dr BT14 | 13 | F10 |
| Glenbank Par BT14 | | |
| *off Leroy St* | 13 | F10 |
| Glenbank Pl BT14 | 13 | F10 |
| Glenbrook Av BT5 | 21 | T17 |
| Glenburn Dr BT14 | 13 | H11 |
| Glenburn Pk BT14 | 14 | K9 |
| Glenbryn Gdns BT14 | 13 | G11 |
| Glenbryn Par BT14 | 13 | G11 |
| Glenbryn Pk BT14 | 13 | H11 |
| Glencairn Cres BT13 | 13 | G12 |
| Glencairn Pas BT13 | 12 | E11 |
| Glencairn Rd BT13 | 12 | E11 |
| Glencairn St BT13 | 13 | G12 |
| Glencairn Wk BT13 | 12 | E11 |
| Glencairn Way BT13 | 12 | E11 |
| Glencoe Pk, New. BT36 | 8 | L4 |
| Glencollyer St BT15 | 14 | M11 |
| Glencourt BT11 | 25 | F19 |
| Glencregagh Ct BT6 | 27 | Q23 |
| Glencregagh Dr BT6 | 27 | R23 |
| Glencregagh Pk BT6 | 27 | R23 |
| Glencregagh Rd BT8 | 27 | R23 |
| Glen Cres BT11 | 25 | F19 |
| Glendale BT10 | 24 | C24 |
| Glendale Av E BT8 | 27 | R24 |
| Glendale Av N BT8 | 27 | R24 |
| Glendale Av S BT8 | 27 | R24 |
| Glendale Av W BT8 | 27 | R24 |
| Glendarragh BT4 | 17 | X11 |
| Glendarragh Ms BT4 | 17 | X10 |
| Glendhu Grn BT4 | 17 | X12 |
| Glendhu Gro BT4 | 16 | W12 |
| Glendhu Manor BT4 | 16 | W11 |
| Glendhu Pk BT4 | 17 | X11 |
| Glendower St BT6 | 27 | R19 |
| Glen Ebor Hts BT4 | | |
| *off Glenmachan Rd* | 17 | Y12 |
| Glen Ebor Pk BT4 | 17 | Y12 |
| Glenfarne St BT13 | | |
| *off Agnes St* | 19 | K13 |
| Glengall La BT12 | | |
| Glengall St BT12 | | |
| *off Glengall St* | 30 | C4 |
| Glengall St BT12 | | |
| *off Glengall St* | 30 | B4 |
| Glengall St BT12 | 30 | B4 |
| Glenhill Ct BT14 | | |
| *off Glenpark St* | 14 | K12 |
| Glenhill Ri BT11 | 24 | E19 |
| Glenholm Av BT8 | 27 | R24 |
| Glenholm Cres BT8 | 27 | R24 |
| Glenholm Pk BT8 | 27 | R24 |
| Glenhoy Dr BT5 | 21 | T17 |
| Glenhoy Ms BT5 | 21 | T17 |
| Glenhurst Ct, New. BT36 | 9 | M4 |
| Glenhurst Dr, New. BT36 | 9 | M4 |

| Street | No. | Grid |
|---|---|---|
| Glenhurst Gdns, New. BT36 | 9 | M4 |
| Glenhurst Par, New. BT36 | 9 | M4 |
| Glenlea Gro BT4 | 17 | X11 |
| Glenlea Pk BT4 | 17 | X12 |
| Glenloch Gdns BT4 | 17 | X11 |
| Glenluce Dr BT4 | 17 | X12 |
| Glenluce Grn BT4 | 17 | X11 |
| Glenluce Wk BT4 | 17 | X11 |
| Glenmachan Av BT4 | 23 | Y13 |
| Glenmachan Dr BT4 | 23 | Y13 |
| Glenmachan Gro BT4 | 23 | Y13 |
| Glenmachan Ms BT4 | 23 | Y13 |
| Glenmachan Pk BT4 | 17 | Y12 |
| Glenmachan Pl BT12 | 19 | H18 |
| Glenmachan Rd BT4 | 17 | Y12 |
| Glenmachan St BT12 | 19 | J18 |
| Glen Manor BT11 | 24 | E19 |
| Glenmillan Dr BT4 | 17 | X12 |
| Glenmillan Pk BT4 | 22 | X13 |
| Glenmore St BT5 | 21 | R16 |
| Glenmurry Ct BT11 | | |
| *off Glen Rd* | 24 | E19 |
| Glen Par BT11 | 25 | F19 |
| Glenpark Ct BT14 | | |
| *off Glenpark St* | 13 | J12 |
| Glenpark St BT14 | 13 | J12 |
| Glenravel St BT15 | | |
| *off Henry Pl* | 20 | M13 |
| Glen Ri BT5 | 28 | W19 |
| Glen Rd BT4 | 23 | Z13 |
| Glen Rd BT5 | 28 | V19 |
| Glen Rd BT11 | 24 | E19 |
| Glen Rd BT12 | | |
| Glen Rd Hts BT11 | 24 | B19 |
| *off Falls Rd* | | |
| Glenrosa Link BT15 | | |
| *off Glenrosa St* | 14 | N12 |
| Glenrosa St BT15 | 14 | M12 |
| Glenrosa St S BT15 | | |
| *off Duncairn Gdns* | 14 | M12 |
| Glenshane Gdns BT11 | 24 | D21 |
| Glensharragh Av BT6 | 28 | T21 |
| Glensharragh Gdns BT6 | 28 | T20 |
| Glensharragh Pk BT6 | 28 | T21 |
| Glenside BT6 | 27 | S22 |
| Glenside Dr BT14 | 13 | F10 |
| Glenside Par BT14 | 13 | F10 |
| Glenside Pk BT14 | 13 | F11 |
| Glentilt St BT13 | | |
| *off Agnes St* | 19 | K13 |
| Glentoran Pl BT6 | | |
| *off Mount St S* | 21 | Q17 |
| Glentoran St BT6 | | |
| *off Mount St S* | 21 | Q17 |
| Glenvale St BT13 | 19 | H13 |
| Glenvarloch St BT5 | 21 | S17 |
| Glenview Av BT5 | 28 | W20 |
| Glenview Ct BT14 | | |
| *off Glenview St* | 14 | K12 |
| Glenview Cres BT5 | 28 | V21 |
| Glenview Dr BT5 | | |
| *off Glenview Gdns* | 28 | W20 |
| Glenview Gdns BT5 | 28 | W20 |
| Glenview Hts BT5 | 28 | V20 |
| Glenview Pk BT5 | 28 | V20 |
| Glenview Rd, Hol. BT18 | 11 | BB7 |
| Glenview St BT14 | 14 | K12 |
| Glenview Ter BT11 | 24 | B22 |
| Glenwherry Pl BT6 | | |
| *off Mount St S* | 21 | Q17 |
| Glenwood Pl BT13 | 19 | J14 |
| Glenwood St BT13 | 19 | J14 |
| Gloucester St BT1 | 31 | E3 |
| Gordon St BT1 | 20 | N14 |
| Gortfin St BT12 | 19 | H16 |
| Gortgrib Dr BT5 | 29 | Z19 |
| Gortin Dr BT5 | 23 | Z17 |
| Gortin Pk BT5 | 23 | Z17 |
| Gortland Av BT5 | 29 | Z19 |
| Gortland Pk BT5 | 29 | Z19 |
| Gortnamona Ct BT11 | | |
| *off Gortnamona Way* | 18 | D18 |
| Gortnamona Hts BT11 | | |
| *off Gortnamona Way* | 18 | D18 |

| Street | No. | Grid |
|---|---|---|
| Gortnamona Pl BT11 | | |
| *off Gortnamona Way* | 18 | D18 |
| Gortnamona Ri BT11 | | |
| *off Gortnamona Way* | 18 | D18 |
| Gortnamona Vw BT11 | | |
| *off Gortnamona Way* | 18 | D18 |
| Gortnamona Way BT11 | 18 | D18 |
| Gotha St BT6 | 21 | Q17 |
| Govan Dr BT5 | 23 | AA18 |
| Governor's Br, The BT7 | 26 | M20 |
| Governor's Br, The BT9 | 26 | M20 |
| Grace Av BT5 | 21 | T17 |
| Gracehill Ct BT14 | 14 | K12 |
| Grace St BT2 | 31 | E4 |
| Grafton St BT13 | | |
| *off Beresford St* | 19 | K14 |
| Graham Gdns BT6 | 27 | S19 |
| Grampian Av BT4 | 21 | T16 |
| Grampian Cl BT4 | 21 | T15 |
| Grampian St BT4 | 21 | T15 |
| Grand Par BT5 | 21 | T18 |
| Grange, The BT4 | 23 | Y13 |
| Grangeville Dr BT10 | | |
| *off Grangeville Gdns* | 24 | E23 |
| Grangeville Gdns BT10 | 24 | E23 |
| Gransha Av BT11 | 24 | E19 |
| Gransha Cres BT11 | 24 | E19 |
| Gransha Dr BT11 | 24 | E19 |
| Gransha Gdns BT11 | 18 | E18 |
| Gransha Grn BT11 | 18 | E18 |
| Gransha Gro BT11 | 24 | E19 |
| Gransha Par BT11 | 24 | E19 |
| Gransha Pk BT11 | 18 | E18 |
| Gransha Ri BT11 | 18 | E18 |
| Gransha Way BT11 | 24 | E19 |
| Granton Pk BT5 | 23 | AA17 |
| Granville Pl BT12 | | |
| *off Servia St* | 19 | K16 |
| Grasmere Gdns BT15 | 8 | K8 |
| Graymount Cres, New. BT36 | 9 | N5 |
| Graymount Dr, New. BT36 | 9 | N5 |
| Graymount Gdns, New. BT36 | 9 | N5 |
| Graymount Gro, New. BT36 | 9 | N5 |
| Graymount Par, New. BT36 | 9 | N5 |
| Graymount Pk, New. BT36 | 9 | N5 |
| Graymount Rd, New. BT36 | 9 | N5 |
| Graymount Ter, New. BT36 | 9 | N5 |
| Grays Ct BT15 | 9 | N5 |
| Grays La BT15 | 9 | M5 |
| Grays La, Hol. BT18 | | |
| *off High St* | 11 | Z6 |
| Great Georges St BT15 | 20 | M13 |
| Great Northern St BT9 | 25 | J20 |
| Great Patrick St BT1 | 20 | M14 |
| Great Victoria St BT2 | 30 | C4 |
| Green, The, Hol. BT18 | 11 | Z8 |
| Greenan BT11 | | |
| *off Rossnareen Rd* | 24 | C20 |
| Greenan Av BT11 | 24 | C21 |
| Greenane Cres BT10 | 24 | C23 |
| Greenane Dr BT10 | 24 | C23 |
| Greencastle Cl, New. BT36 | 9 | N5 |
| Greencastle Pl BT15 | 9 | N6 |
| Green Cres BT5 | 22 | W16 |
| Greenhill Gro BT14 | | |
| *off Wolfend Dr* | 13 | F9 |
| Greenhill La BT14 | 13 | F9 |
| Greenland St BT13 | 20 | L14 |
| Greenlea Gdns BT5 | | |
| *off Whincroft Rd* | 28 | W19 |
| Green Mt BT5 | 28 | W19 |
| Greenmount Pl BT15 | | |
| *off Glenrosa St* | 14 | N12 |
| Greenmount St BT15 | | |
| *off North Queen St* | 14 | N12 |
| Greenore St BT6 | 21 | R18 |
| Green Rd BT5 | 22 | W16 |
| Greenview St BT9 | 25 | H24 |

Iveagh Par BT12 19 H17
Iveagh St BT12 19 H17
Iverna Cl BT12 19 K17
Iverna St BT12 19 K17

**J**

Jacksons Rd, Hol. BT18 11 Y8
Jackson St BT13
*off North*
*Boundary St* 20 L14
Jamaica Ct BT14 13 J11
Jamaica Rd BT14 13 J11
Jamaica St BT14 13 J11
Jamaica Way BT14 13 J11
James Ct BT15
*off Kansas Av Flats* 14 L10
Jameson St BT7 27 P20
James's Pas BT7
*off Ormeau Rd* 31 E6
James St S BT2 30 C4
Jellicoe Av BT15 14 M11
Jellicoe Dr BT15 14 M10
Jellicoe Par BT15 14 N10
Jellicoe Pk BT15 14 M10
Jennymount St BT15 14 N11
Jersey Pl BT13
*off Jersey St* 19 K13
Jersey St BT13 19 K13
Jerusalem St BT7 26 N19
Jetty Rd BT3 16 U9
Joanmount Dr BT14 13 H9
Joanmount Gdns BT14 13 H9
Joanmount Pk BT14 13 H9
Jocelyn Av BT6 21 R17
Jocelyn Gdns BT6 21 R17
Jocelyn St BT6 21 R17
Johnston Ct BT5 22 X16
John St BT12 30 B2
Jonesboro Pk BT5 21 S17
Joys Entry BT1
*off Ann St* 31 E2
Joy St BT2 31 E5
Jubilee Av BT15 14 L11
Jubilee Rd BT9 20 L18
Jude St BT12 19 K15
Julia St BT4 21 S15

**K**

Kane St BT13 19 J15
Kansas Av BT15 14 L10
Kansas Av Flats BT15 14 L10
Kashmir Rd BT13 19 H15
Kathleen Ct BT5 21 R15
Keadyville Av BT15 14 N10
Keatley St BT5 21 R16
Kells Av BT11 24 B22
Kelvin Par BT14 14 K10
Kenard Av BT11 24 C20
Kenbaan Ct BT5
*off Trillick St* 21 R16
Kenbaan St BT5
*off Beersbridge Rd* 21 R17
Kenbella Par BT15
*off Salisbury Av* 14 L9
Kendal St BT13 19 K14
Kenilworth Pl BT4
*off Ballymacarrett*
*Rd* 21 Q15
Kenmare Pk BT12 30 B5
Kennedy Way BT11 24 E19
Kennel Br BT4 22 X13
Kensington Av BT5 21 T17
Kensington Ct BT5 22 X18
Kensington Dr BT5 23 Y18
Kensington Gdns BT5 22 X18
Kensington Gdns S BT5 22 X18
Kensington Gdns W
BT5 22 X18
Kensington Gate BT5 22 X18
Kensington Manor BT5 23 Y18
Kensington Pk BT5 22 X18
Kensington Rd BT5 22 X18
Kensington St BT12 30 C6
Kent St BT1 20 M14
Kernan Cl, New. BT36
*off Ballyroney Hill* 9 M4
Kerrera Ct BT14
*off Kerrera St* 13 H12

Kerrera Ms BT14
*off Kerrera St* 13 H12
Kerrera St BT14 13 H12
Kerrington Ct BT9
*off Marlborough Pk S* 26 K21
Kerrsland Cres BT5 22 V16
Kerrsland Dr BT5 22 V16
Kerrsland Ms BT5 22 V16
Kerrsland Par BT5 22 V16
Keswick St BT13 19 J13
Keylands Pl BT2
*off Amelia St* 30 C4
Kilbroney Bend BT6 27 S21
Kilburn St BT12 19 J18
Kilcoole Gdns BT14 8 H7
Kilcoole Pk BT14 8 H7
Kildare Pl BT13 20 M14
Kildare St BT13 20 M14
Kilhorne Gdns BT5 22 X18
Killagan Bend BT6 27 R20
Killard Pl BT10 25 F24
Killarn Cl BT6 28 U20
Killeen Pk BT11 24 D21
Killowen St BT6 21 R18
Kilmakee Pk BT5 29 AA19
Kilmore Cl BT13 19 J15
Kilmore Sq BT13 19 J15
Kilmory Gdns BT5 23 AA18
Kimberley Dr BT7 26 N21
Kimberley St BT7 26 N20
Kimona Dr BT4 21 T14
Kimona St BT4 21 T14
Kimscourt BT5 22 X18
Kinallen Ct BT7 26 N19
Kinallen St BT7
*off Kinallen Ct* 26 N19
Kinbane Way BT10 25 F24
Kincora Av BT4 22 V16
Kincora Ms BT4 22 V16
Kincraig Av BT5 23 AA18
Kinedar Cres BT4 22 W15
Kingsberry Pk BT6 27 Q22
Kings Brae BT5 23 Z17
King's Br BT7 26 N20
King's Br BT9 26 N20
Kings Ct BT10 25 G23
Kings Ct BT15
*off Lancaster St* 20 M14
Kingscourt Av BT6
*off Euston St* 21 R17
Kingscourt Cl BT6 21 R17
Kingscourt Cres BT6 21 R17
Kings Cres BT5 22 X17
Kingsdale Pk BT5 23 Y17
Kingsden Pk BT5 22 W18
Kings Dr BT5 22 X17
Kingsland Dr BT5 23 Z18
Kingsland Pk BT5 23 Z18
Kingsleigh BT5 22 W17
Kingsley Ct BT4 22 V15
Kings Link BT5 23 Z17
Kings Manor BT5 23 Y17
Kingsmere Av BT14 13 J10
Kings Pk BT5 22 X17
Kings Pk La BT5 22 W17
Kings Rd BT5 22 W17
Kings Sq BT5 23 Y17
Kingston Ct BT14
*off Jamaica Rd* 13 J11
King St BT1 30 C2
King St Ms BT1 30 B2
Kings Vale BT5 22 W17
Kingsway Av BT5 23 Y18
Kingsway Cl BT5 23 Y18
Kingsway Dr BT5 23 Y17
Kingsway Gdns BT5 23 Y18
Kingsway Pk BT5 23 Y18
Kingswood Pk BT5 23 Z18
Kingswood St BT5 21 R16
Kinnaird Cl BT14 14 L12
Kinnaird Pl BT14 14 L12
Kinnaird St BT14 20 L13
Kinnaird Terrace BT14 20 L13
Kinnaird Ter BT14
*off Kinnaird Pl* 20 L13
Kinnegar Av, Hol. BT18 11 Y6
Kinnegar Ct, Hol. BT18 11 Y6
Kinnegar Dr, Hol. BT18 11 Y6

Kinnegar Rd BT10 25 F24
Kinnegar Rd, Hol.
BT18 11 Y6
Kinross Av BT5 23 AA17
Kirk Cres BT13
*off Kirk St* 19 H15
Kirkliston Dr BT5 22 U16
Kirkliston Gdns BT5 22 V17
Kirkliston Pk BT5 22 U17
Kirklowe Dr BT10 24 E24
Kirk St BT13 19 H14
Kirn Pk BT5 23 AA18
Kitchener Dr BT12 19 J18
Kitchener St BT12 19 J18
Klondyke St BT13 19 K14
Knightsbridge Manor
BT9 26 L23
Knightsbridge Ms BT9 26 L22
Knightsbridge Pk BT9 26 L23
Knights Grn BT6 27 S19
Knockbracken Pk BT6 27 Q22
Knockbreda Dr BT6 27 Q22
Knockbreda Gdns BT6 27 Q22
Knockbreda Pk BT6 27 Q22
Knockbreda Pk Ms BT6 27 Q22
Knockbreda Rd BT6 27 P22
Knockburn Pk BT5 23 Z16
Knockcastle Pk BT5 22 X18
Knockdarragh Pk BT4 23 Y13
Knockdene Pk BT5 22 X17
Knockdene Pk N BT5 22 X16
Knockdene Pk S BT5 22 X16
Knockdhu Pk BT11 24 C20
Knock Eden Cres BT6 27 Q21
Knock Eden Dr BT6 27 Q21
Knock Eden Gro BT6 27 Q21
Knock Eden Par BT6 27 Q21
Knock Eden Pk BT6 27 Q21
Knock Grn BT5 28 W19
Knock Gro BT5 28 V19
Knockhill Pk BT5 22 W16
Knockland Pk BT5 23 Z17
Knock Link BT5 22 W18
Knocklofty Ct BT4 22 W15
Knocklofty Pk BT4 22 W15
Knockmarloch Pk BT4 23 Y13
Knockmount Gdns BT5 22 W18
Knockmount Pk BT5 22 W18
Knocknagoney Av BT4 17 X11
Knocknagoney Dale
BT4
*off Knocknagoney*
*Rd* 16 W11
Knocknagoney Dr BT4 17 X11
Knocknagoney Gdns
BT4 17 X11
Knocknagoney Grn BT4 17 X11
Knocknagoney Gro BT4 17 X11
Knocknagoney Pk BT4 16 W11
Knocknagoney Rd BT4 16 W11
Knocknagoney Way
BT4
*off Knocknagoney Av* 17 X11
Knock Rd BT5 28 V20
Knocktern Gdns BT4 22 X16
Knockvale Gro BT5 22 W17
Knockvale Pk BT5 22 W17
Knock Way BT5 28 W19
Knockwood Cres BT5 22 V18
Knockwood Dr BT5 22 W18
Knockwood Gro BT5 22 W18
Knockwood Pk BT5 22 V18
Knutsford Dr BT14 14 K10
Koram Ring BT11
*off South Link* 24 E20
Kylemore Pk BT14 8 J8
Kyle St BT4 21 T14

**L**

Laburnum Ct BT5 21 T16
Laburnum La BT5 21 T16
*off Bloomfield Av*
Laburnum St BT5 21 T16
Lackagh Ct BT4 21 Q15
Ladas Dr BT6 27 S20
Ladas Wk BT6 27 S19
Ladas Way BT6 27 S19
Ladbrook Dr BT14 13 H12

Ladybrook Av BT11 24 C22
Ladybrook Cres BT11 24 C22
Ladybrook Cross BT11 24 C23
Ladybrook Dr BT11 24 D22
Ladybrook Gdns BT11 24 C22
Ladybrook Gro BT11 24 D22
Ladybrook Par BT11 24 C22
Ladybrook Pk BT11 24 C22
Ladymar Ct BT12
*off Lady St* 19 K16
Ladymar Gro BT12
*off Lady St* 19 K16
Ladymar Pk BT12
*off Lady St* 19 K16
Ladymar Wk BT12
*off Lady St* 19 K16
Ladymar Way BT12
*off Lady St* 19 K16
Lady St BT12 19 K16
Laganbank Rd BT1 31 G3
Lagan Br BT1 20 P14
Lagan Br BT3 20 P14
Laganvale Ct BT9 26 M22
Laganvale Manor BT9 26 M22
Laganvale St BT9 26 M21
Laganview Ct BT1 31 G2
Laganview Ms BT5 31 G2
Lake Glen Av BT11 25 F19
Lake Glen Cl BT11 25 F19
Lake Glen Cres BT11 24 E19
Lake Glen Dr BT11 24 E19
Lake Glen Grn BT11 25 F19
Lake Glen Par BT11
*off Lake Glen Dr* 25 F19
Lake Glen Pk BT11 24 E19
Lanark Way BT13 19 H14
Lancaster St BT15 20 M14
Lancaster Ter BT15
*off Lancaster St* 20 M14
Lancedean Rd BT6 27 S22
Lancefield Rd BT9 25 J21
Landscape Ter BT14 19 K13
Landseer St BT9 26 M19
Langholm Row BT5
*off Granton Pk* 23 AA17
Langley St BT13
*off Tennent St* 19 J13
Langtry Ct BT5 21 R16
Lansdowne Dr BT15 9 M8
Lansdowne Ms BT15 9 M7
Lansdowne Pk BT15 9 M8
Lansdowne Pk N BT15 9 M7
Lansdowne Rd BT15 9 M7
Lanyon Pl BT1 31 G3
Larch Cl, Hol. BT18
*off Loughview Av* 11 Z8
Larch St BT5
*off Trillick St* 21 R16
Larkfield Ct BT4
*off Larkfield Rd* 22 U14
Larkfield Dr BT4 21 T13
Larkfield Gdns BT4 22 U14
Larkfield Gro BT4 22 U14
Larkfield Manor BT4 21 T14
Larkfield Pk BT4 22 U14
Larkfield Rd BT4 22 U14
Larkstone St BT9
*off Lisburn Rd* 25 H21
La Salle Dr BT12 19 H17
La Salle Gdns BT12 19 H17
La Salle Ms BT12
*off La Salle Dr* 19 H17
La Salle Pk BT12 19 H17
Laurelvale BT4 22 W15
Laurel Wd BT8 26 N23
Lavens Dr BT14 13 F10
Lavinia Ms BT7 20 N18
Lavinia Sq BT7 20 N18
Lawnbrook Av BT13 19 J15
Lawnbrook Ct BT13 19 J15
Lawnbrook Dr BT13
Lawnbrook Sq BT13 19 J14
*off Lawnbrook Av*
Lawnbrook Way BT13 19 J15
Lawnmount St BT6 21 Q17
Lawnview St BT13 19 H14
Lawrence St BT7 20 M18

| Street | Page | Grid |
|---|---|---|
| Laws Ct BT1 | 20 | M14 |
| Lawther Ct BT15 | 14 | M11 |
| Lawyer Gdns BT12 *off Linfield Rd* | 30 | B5 |
| Lead Hill BT6 | 28 | V20 |
| Lead Hill Pk BT6 | 28 | V20 |
| Lead Hill Vw BT6 | 28 | V20 |
| Lecale St BT12 | 19 | J18 |
| Ledley Hall Cl BT5 *off Beersbridge Rd* | 21 | S17 |
| Leeson St BT12 | 19 | K16 |
| Leestone Ter BT11 *off Kells Av* | 24 | B22 |
| Legann St BT14 | 13 | F10 |
| Leganoe St BT14 | 12 | E9 |
| Leggagh Ct BT14 | 13 | F10 |
| Leginn St BT14 | 12 | E9 |
| Legmail St BT14 *off Crumlin Rd* | 13 | F10 |
| Legnavea St BT14 | 12 | E9 |
| Legoniel Pl BT14 | 12 | E9 |
| Leitrim St BT6 | 21 | R17 |
| Lelia St BT4 | 21 | S15 |
| Lemberg St BT12 | 19 | J17 |
| Lemonfield Av, Hol. BT18 | 11 | AA7 |
| Lenadoon Av BT11 | 24 | B21 |
| Lenadoon Wk BT11 | 24 | B22 |
| Lena St BT5 | 21 | T16 |
| Lendrick St BT5 | 21 | R15 |
| Lennox Av BT8 | 27 | Q24 |
| Lennoxvale BT9 | 26 | L20 |
| Leopold Gdns BT13 | 19 | H13 |
| Leopold Pk BT13 | 19 | H13 |
| Leopold Pl BT13 | 19 | J13 |
| Leoville St BT13 *off Kashmir Rd* | 19 | H15 |
| Lepper St BT13 | 20 | M13 |
| Leroy St BT14 | 13 | F10 |
| Leven Cl BT5 *off Leven Dr* | 23 | AA18 |
| Leven Cres BT5 | 23 | AA18 |
| Leven Dr BT5 | 23 | AA18 |
| Leven Pk BT5 | 23 | AA18 |
| Leven Pl BT5 *off Leven Dr* | 23 | AA18 |
| Lever St BT14 | 12 | E8 |
| Lewis Av BT4 | 21 | S15 |
| Lewis Ct BT6 | 21 | R17 |
| Lewis Dr BT4 | 21 | S15 |
| Lewis Gdns BT4 | 21 | S15 |
| Lewis Ms BT4 | 21 | S15 |
| Lewis Pk BT4 | 21 | S15 |
| Library Ct BT4 | 22 | W16 |
| Library St BT1 | 20 | M14 |
| Lichfield Av BT5 | 21 | T17 |
| Liffey St BT4 *off Shannon St* | 14 | K12 |
| Ligoniel Pl BT14 | 12 | E9 |
| Ligoniel Rd BT14 | 12 | E8 |
| Lille Pk BT10 | 24 | E24 |
| Lilliput Ct BT15 *off Clanmorris St* | 14 | N12 |
| Lime Ct BT13 | 20 | L14 |
| Limegrove BT15 | 9 | M5 |
| Limehill Gdns BT14 *off Leginn St* | 13 | F9 |
| Limehill St BT14 | 12 | E9 |
| Limepark Ms BT14 *off Lavens Dr* | 13 | F10 |
| Limepark St BT14 *off Lavens Dr* | 13 | F10 |
| Limestone Rd BT15 | 14 | L11 |
| Limewood Gro BT4 *off Kincora Av* | 22 | W15 |
| Lincoln Av BT14 | 20 | L13 |
| Lincoln Pl BT12 | 30 | C4 |
| Lincoln Sq BT12 *off Abyssinia St* | 19 | K16 |
| Linden Gdns BT14 | 14 | K11 |
| Lindsay Ct BT7 *off Lindsay St* | 31 | E5 |
| Lindsay St BT7 | 30 | D5 |
| Lindsay Way BT7 | 31 | E5 |
| Linen Ct BT5 | 21 | T17 |
| Linen Gdns BT5 | 21 | T17 |
| Linen Gro BT14 | 13 | F9 |
| Linen Hall St BT2 | 30 | D3 |
| Linen Hall St W BT2 | 30 | D4 |
| Linfield Av BT12 *off Linfield Rd* | 30 | B5 |
| Linfield Dr BT12 *off Linfield Rd* | 30 | B4 |
| Linfield Gdns BT12 *off Linfield Rd* | 30 | B5 |
| Linfield Rd BT12 | 30 | B5 |
| Linfield St BT12 *off Linfield Rd* | 30 | B5 |
| Linview Ct BT12 *off Excise Wk* | 19 | K16 |
| Lisavon Dr BT4 | 21 | T14 |
| Lisavon Ms BT4 | 21 | T14 |
| Lisavon Par BT4 | 21 | T14 |
| Lisavon St BT4 | 21 | T14 |
| Lisbon St BT5 | 21 | Q16 |
| Lisbreen Pk BT15 | 8 | L8 |
| Lisburn Av BT9 | 25 | J20 |
| Lisburn Rd BT9 | 25 | H22 |
| Lisdarragh Pk BT14 | 8 | K8 |
| Lisfaddan Cres BT12 | 30 | A2 |
| Lisfaddan Dr BT12 | 30 | A2 |
| Lisfaddan Pl BT12 | 30 | A2 |
| Lisfaddan Way BT12 | 30 | A2 |
| Lislea Av BT9 *off Lisburn Rd* | 25 | H21 |
| Lislea Dr BT9 | 25 | H21 |
| Lisleen Rd BT5 | 29 | Z21 |
| Lismain St BT6 | 21 | R18 |
| Lismore St BT6 | 21 | Q17 |
| Lismoyne Pk BT15 | 8 | L7 |
| Lisnasharragh Pk BT6 | 28 | U21 |
| Lisnasharragh Ter BT6 *off Lisnasharragh Pk* | 28 | U21 |
| Lissan Cl BT6 | 27 | R21 |
| Lissan Link BT6 *off Lissan Cl* | 27 | R21 |
| Lisvarna Hts BT12 | 19 | K16 |
| Lisvarna Pl BT12 | 19 | K16 |
| Little Charlotte St BT7 | 31 | E6 |
| Little Donegall St BT1 | 20 | M14 |
| Little Georges St BT15 *off Henry St* | 20 | M13 |
| Little Grosvenor St BT12 *off Burnaby Pl* | 19 | K16 |
| Little May St BT2 | 31 | E3 |
| Little Patrick St BT15 | 20 | N14 |
| Little Victoria St BT2 | 30 | C4 |
| Little York St BT15 | 20 | N14 |
| Locan St BT12 | 19 | H16 |
| Lochinver Dr BT5 | 23 | AA18 |
| Lockside Ct BT9 | 26 | M21 |
| Locksley Dr BT10 | 25 | F23 |
| Locksley Gdns BT10 | 25 | F24 |
| Locksley Gra BT10 | 25 | F23 |
| Locksley Par BT10 | 25 | F24 |
| Locksley Pk BT10 | 25 | F23 |
| Locksley Pl BT10 *off Locksley Pk* | 25 | F23 |
| Lockview Rd BT9 | 26 | M21 |
| Lombard St BT1 | 30 | D1 |
| Lomond Av BT4 | 21 | T15 |
| Lomond St BT4 | 21 | T15 |
| London Rd BT6 | 21 | Q18 |
| London St BT6 | 21 | Q17 |
| Longacre BT8 | 27 | P23 |
| Loopland Cres BT6 | 21 | R18 |
| Loopland Dr BT6 | 21 | R18 |
| Loopland Gdns BT6 | 21 | S18 |
| Loopland Gro BT6 | 21 | S18 |
| Loopland Par BT6 *off Loopland Pk* | 21 | S18 |
| Loopland Pk BT6 | 21 | S18 |
| Loopland Rd BT6 | 21 | S18 |
| Lord St BT5 | 21 | R16 |
| Lord St Ms BT5 *off Lord St* | 21 | R17 |
| Lorne St BT9 | 26 | K19 |
| Lothair Av BT15 | 14 | L11 |
| Lothian Av BT5 | 23 | AA18 |
| Louden St BT13 | 30 | A1 |
| Lough Lea BT5 | 21 | Q15 |
| Loughrey Ct BT15 | 14 | L10 |
| Loughview BT14 | 13 | G8 |
| Loughview Av, Hol. BT18 | 11 | Z8 |
| Loughview Cl BT14 | 13 | G8 |
| Loughview Dr BT6 | 27 | R23 |
| Loughview Glen BT14 | 13 | G8 |
| Loughview Grn BT14 | 13 | G8 |
| Loughview Hts BT14 | 13 | G8 |
| Loughview Manor BT14 | 13 | G8 |
| Loughview Meadows BT14 | 13 | G8 |
| Loughview St BT14 *off Crumlin Rd* | 13 | F10 |
| Loughview Ter BT15 | 14 | N10 |
| Louisa Ct BT14 | 14 | K12 |
| Lovatt St BT5 *off Ravenscroft Av* | 21 | T16 |
| Lower Braniel Rd BT5 | 28 | W20 |
| Lower Clara Cres BT5 *off Clara Av* | 21 | T17 |
| Lower Clonard St BT12 | 19 | J16 |
| Lower Ctyd BT7 | 26 | N21 |
| Lower Cres BT7 | 20 | M18 |
| Lower Garfield St BT1 | 30 | D1 |
| Lower Kilburn St BT12 | 19 | J17 |
| Lower Mt St BT5 *off Mount St* | 21 | Q16 |
| Lower Regent St BT13 | 20 | M14 |
| Lower Rockview St BT12 | 19 | J17 |
| Lower Stanfield St BT7 | 31 | F4 |
| Lower Windsor Av BT9 | 25 | J19 |
| Lowland Av BT5 | 23 | AA18 |
| Lowland Gdns BT5 *off Lowland Av* | 23 | AA18 |
| Lowland Wk BT5 *off Kilmory Gdns* | 23 | AA18 |
| Lowry Ct BT6 | 27 | P23 |
| Lowwood Gdns BT15 | 9 | N7 |
| Lowwood Pk BT15 | 9 | M7 |
| Lucerne Par BT9 | 26 | M21 |
| Lucknow St BT13 *off Cupar St* | 19 | H15 |
| Ludlow Sq BT15 | 20 | M13 |
| Lupus Gro BT14 | 13 | F9 |
| Luxembourg Ct BT15 | 14 | L9 |
| Luxor Gdns BT5 | 21 | T17 |
| Lyle Ct BT13 *off Agnes St* | 19 | K13 |
| Lyndhurst Av BT13 | 18 | E13 |
| Lyndhurst Cl BT13 | 18 | F13 |
| Lyndhurst Ct BT13 | 18 | E13 |
| Lyndhurst Cres BT13 | 18 | E13 |
| Lyndhurst Dr BT13 | 18 | F13 |
| Lyndhurst Gdns BT13 | 18 | F13 |
| Lyndhurst Gro BT13 | 18 | E13 |
| Lyndhurst Hts BT13 | 18 | E13 |
| Lyndhurst Link BT13 | 18 | F13 |
| Lyndhurst Meadows BT13 | 18 | E13 |
| Lyndhurst Par BT13 | 18 | F13 |
| Lyndhurst Pk BT13 | 18 | F13 |
| Lyndhurst Path BT13 | 18 | E13 |
| Lyndhurst Pl BT13 | 18 | F13 |
| Lyndhurst Row BT13 | 18 | E13 |
| Lyndhurst Vw Av BT13 | 18 | E13 |
| Lyndhurst Vw Cl BT13 | 18 | E13 |
| Lyndhurst Vw Pk BT13 | 18 | E13 |
| Lyndhurst Vw Rd BT13 | 18 | E13 |
| Lyndhurst Way BT13 | 18 | F13 |
| Lynwood Pk, Hol. BT18 | 11 | AA7 |

## M

| Street | Page | Grid |
|---|---|---|
| Mabel Ct BT12 | 30 | A6 |
| Mabel St BT12 *off Utility St* | 30 | A6 |
| McAdam Gdns BT12 *off Linfield Rd* | 30 | B5 |
| McAdam Pk BT12 | 30 | B5 |
| McAllister St BT4 *off Mersey St* | 21 | S15 |
| McAllister Ms BT4 *off Mersey St* | 21 | S15 |
| McArthur Ct BT4 | 21 | R15 |
| Macart St BT13 | 20 | P14 |
| McAuley St BT7 | 31 | F5 |
| McCandless St BT13 | 19 | J13 |
| McCaughan Pk BT6 | 28 | T21 |
| McCaughey Rd BT3 | 15 | Q12 |
| McCavanas Pl BT2 | 30 | D4 |
| McCleery St BT15 *off North Hill St* | 20 | M13 |
| McClintock St BT2 | 30 | C4 |
| McClure St BT7 | 20 | M18 |
| McDonnell Ct BT12 *off Servia St* | 19 | K16 |
| McDonnell St BT12 | 19 | K16 |
| McIvor's Pl BT13 *off Brown St* | 30 | C1 |
| Mackey St BT15 | 14 | M12 |
| McKibben's Ct BT1 *off North St* | 20 | M14 |
| McMaster St BT5 | 21 | R15 |
| McMullans La BT6 | 21 | Q17 |
| McQuillan St BT13 *off Colligan St* | 19 | J16 |
| Madison Av BT13 | 14 | L10 |
| Madison Av E BT4 | 21 | T15 |
| Madras St BT13 | 19 | J13 |
| Madrid Ct BT5 *off Madrid St* | 21 | Q16 |
| Madrid St BT5 | 21 | Q16 |
| Magdala St BT7 | 20 | M18 |
| Maghies Pl BT6 *off Pearl St* | 21 | R17 |
| Majestic Dr BT12 | 30 | B6 |
| Major St BT5 | 21 | R15 |
| Malcolmson St BT13 | 19 | J16 |
| Maldon Ct BT12 | 19 | J17 |
| Maldon St BT12 | 19 | J17 |
| Malfin Dr BT9 | 25 | G24 |
| Malinmore Pk BT11 | 24 | B22 |
| Malone Av BT9 | 26 | K19 |
| Malone Beeches BT9 *off Norton Dr* | 25 | J23 |
| Malone Chase BT9 | 26 | L20 |
| Malone Ct BT9 | 25 | J23 |
| Malone Ct Ms BT9 *off Malone Ct* | 25 | J23 |
| Malone Gra BT9 | 26 | K23 |
| Malone Hill Pk BT9 | 25 | J23 |
| Malone Meadows BT9 | 25 | J24 |
| Malone Pk BT9 | 25 | H22 |
| Malone Pk Cen BT9 | 25 | J23 |
| Malone Pk La BT9 | 25 | H22 |
| Malone Pl BT12 | 20 | L18 |
| Malton Dr BT9 | 25 | G24 |
| Malton Fold BT9 | 25 | G24 |
| Malvern Cl BT13 | 19 | K13 |
| Malvern Pl BT13 *off Malvern St* | 20 | L14 |
| Malvern St BT13 | 20 | L14 |
| Malvern Way BT13 | 20 | L14 |
| Malwood Cl BT9 *off Finwood Pk* | 25 | G24 |
| Manderson St BT4 | 21 | S15 |
| Manna Gro BT5 | 21 | T18 |
| Mann's Rd BT5 | 29 | AA21 |
| Manor, The BT10 | 24 | C24 |
| Manor Cl BT14 | 14 | L12 |
| Manor Ct BT14 | 14 | K12 |
| Manor Dr BT14 | 14 | K12 |
| Manor Ms BT10 | 24 | C24 |
| Manor St BT14 | 14 | K12 |
| Mansfield St BT13 *off Downing St* | 19 | K14 |
| Maple Ct, Hol. BT18 *off Loughview Av* | 11 | Z8 |
| Mara Gdns, Hol. BT18 *off Strand Av* | 11 | Z5 |
| Maralin Pl BT15 *off Sheridan St* | 20 | M13 |
| Marchioness Grn BT12 *off Marchioness St* | 19 | K16 |
| Marchioness St BT12 | 19 | K16 |
| March St BT13 | 19 | H14 |
| Marcus Ward St BT7 | 30 | D5 |
| Marfield St BT4 *off St. Leonards St* | 21 | R15 |
| Marguerite Pk BT10 | 25 | F23 |
| Marina Pk BT5 | 28 | U19 |
| Marine Par, Hol. BT18 | 11 | Z5 |
| Marino Pk, Hol. BT18 | 11 | BB4 |
| Market St BT1 | 31 | F3 |
| Market St BT7 | 31 | F4 |

|  | | |
|---|---|---|
| Marlborough Av BT9 | | |
| *off Lisburn Av* | 25 | J20 |
| Marlborough Ct BT1 | | |
| *off Queens Sq* | 31 | F1 |
| Marlborough Ct BT9 | | |
| *off Lisburn Rd* | 25 | J20 |
| Marlborough Gdns BT9 | 26 | K21 |
| Marlborough Gate BT9 | 26 | K21 |
| Marlborough Hts BT6 | 28 | U21 |
| Marlborough Pk BT9 | 26 | K21 |
| Marlborough Pk Cen BT9 | 25 | J21 |
| Marlborough Pk Cross Av BT9 | 26 | K21 |
| Marlborough Pk N BT9 | 25 | J20 |
| Marlborough Pk S BT9 | 25 | J21 |
| Marlborough Pk St BT1 | 31 | F1 |
| Marlfield Dr BT5 | 29 | X19 |
| Marlfield Ri BT5 | 29 | Y19 |
| Marmont Cres BT4 | 16 | W12 |
| Marmont Dr BT4 | 16 | W12 |
| Marmont Pk BT4 | 16 | W12 |
| Marmount Gdns BT14 | 13 | H10 |
| Marquis St BT1 | 30 | C2 |
| Marsden Gdns BT15 | 14 | L10 |
| Marsden Gdns Flats BT15 | | |
| *off Marsden Gdns* | 14 | L10 |
| Marsden Ter BT15 | | |
| *off Marsden Gdns* | 14 | L10 |
| Marshalls Rd BT5 | 28 | T19 |
| Marshall St BT1 | | |
| *off Dunbar St* | 20 | N14 |
| Martello Ter, Hol. BT18 | 11 | AA6 |
| Martinez Av BT5 | 21 | T16 |
| Martin St BT5 | 21 | R16 |
| Marylebone Pk BT9 | 26 | M22 |
| Maryville Av BT9 | 25 | J20 |
| Maryville Ct BT7 | | |
| *off Maryville St* | 30 | D5 |
| Maryville Pk BT9 | 25 | H21 |
| Maryville St BT7 | 30 | D6 |
| Mashona Ct BT6 | 21 | R18 |
| Massareene Path BT12 | | |
| *off Cullingtree Rd* | 19 | K16 |
| Massey Av BT4 | 23 | Y14 |
| Massey Ct BT4 | 23 | Z14 |
| Massey Grn BT4 | 23 | Y14 |
| Massey Pk BT4 | 23 | Z14 |
| Matchett St BT13 | 19 | J13 |
| Matilda Av BT12 | 30 | B6 |
| Matilda Dr BT12 | 30 | B6 |
| Matilda Gdns BT12 | 30 | A6 |
| Mawhinneys Ct BT13 | | |
| *off Melbourne St* | 30 | B1 |
| Maxwells Pl BT12 | | |
| *off Maxwell St* | 30 | B6 |
| Maxwell St BT12 | 30 | B6 |
| Mayfair Av BT6 | 27 | S20 |
| Mayfair Ct BT14 | | |
| *off Ardilea St* | 14 | K12 |
| Mayfield Cl BT10 | 24 | C23 |
| Mayfield Sq BT10 | 24 | C23 |
| Mayfield St BT9 | 25 | J20 |
| Mayflower St BT5 | 21 | S17 |
| Maymount St BT6 | 21 | Q17 |
| Mayo Ct BT13 | 19 | H14 |
| Mayo Link BT13 | | |
| *off Mayo St* | 19 | H14 |
| Mayo Pk BT13 | 19 | H14 |
| Mayo Pl BT13 | 19 | H14 |
| Mayo St BT13 | 19 | H14 |
| Mays Meadow BT1 | 31 | G3 |
| May St BT1 | 31 | E3 |
| Meadowbank Pl BT9 | 25 | J19 |
| Meadowbank St BT9 | 26 | K19 |
| Meadow Cl BT15 | 14 | M12 |
| Meadow Pl BT15 | 14 | M12 |
| Medway Ct BT4 | | |
| *off Medway St* | 21 | R15 |
| Medway St BT4 | 21 | R15 |
| Meekon St BT4 | 21 | S15 |
| Melbourne Ct BT13 | | |
| *off Melbourne St* | 30 | B1 |
| Melbourne St BT13 | 30 | B2 |
| Melfort Dr BT5 | 23 | Z18 |
| Melrose Av BT5 | 21 | T16 |
| Melrose St BT9 | 26 | K19 |
| Meridi St BT12 | 19 | J17 |
| Merkland Pl BT13 | 19 | H15 |
| Merkland St BT13 | 19 | H15 |
| Merok Cres BT6 | 28 | T20 |
| Merok Dr BT6 | 28 | T20 |
| Merok Gdns BT6 | 28 | T21 |
| Merok Pk BT6 | 28 | T21 |
| Merryfield Dr BT15 | 8 | K8 |
| Mersey St BT4 | 21 | S15 |
| Merston Gdns, New. BT36 | 9 | M4 |
| Mervue Ct BT15 | 14 | M12 |
| Mervue St BT15 | 14 | M12 |
| Meyrick Pk BT14 | 8 | H8 |
| Mica Dr BT12 | 19 | G16 |
| Mica St BT12 | 19 | H16 |
| Middle Braniel Rd BT5 | 29 | X22 |
| Middlepath St BT5 | 31 | G1 |
| Midland Cl BT15 | 14 | N12 |
| Midland Cres BT15 | | |
| *off Midland Cl* | 14 | N12 |
| Midland Ter BT15 | 14 | N12 |
| Mileriver St BT15 | 14 | M11 |
| Milewater Rd BT3 | 15 | P11 |
| Milewater St BT15 | 14 | N12 |
| Milford Pl BT12 | 30 | A2 |
| Milford Ri BT12 | 30 | A2 |
| Milford St BT12 | 30 | A2 |
| Milk St BT5 | | |
| *off Bloomfield Av* | 21 | T16 |
| Millar St BT6 | 21 | Q18 |
| Mill Av BT14 | 12 | E8 |
| Millbank Pk BT14 | | |
| *off Wolfend Dr* | 13 | F9 |
| Millennium Way BT12 | 19 | G16 |
| Millfield BT1 | 30 | C1 |
| Mill Pond Ct BT5 | 21 | S16 |
| Mill St W BT13 | 19 | J13 |
| Milltown Row BT12 | 19 | G18 |
| Mill Valley Av BT14 | 12 | E9 |
| Mill Valley Cl BT14 | 12 | E10 |
| Mill Valley Cres BT14 | 12 | E10 |
| Mill Valley Dr BT14 | 12 | E10 |
| Mill Valley La BT14 | 12 | E10 |
| Mill Valley N BT14 | 12 | E10 |
| Mill Valley Pl BT14 | 12 | E10 |
| Mill Valley Rd BT14 | 12 | E10 |
| Millview Ct BT14 | 13 | F9 |
| Milner St BT12 | 19 | J17 |
| Minds Way BT9 | 20 | L18 |
| Mineral St BT15 | 14 | N10 |
| Mizen Gdns BT11 | 24 | B21 |
| Moffatt St BT15 | 20 | M13 |
| Moira Ct BT5 | 21 | Q16 |
| Moltke St BT12 | 19 | J18 |
| Molyneaux St BT15 | | |
| *off Henry St* | 20 | N13 |
| Monagh Cres BT11 | 18 | D18 |
| Monagh Dr BT11 | 18 | D17 |
| Monagh Gro BT11 | 18 | D18 |
| Monagh Link BT11 | 18 | D18 |
| Monagh Par BT11 | 18 | D17 |
| Monagh Rd BT11 | 18 | D18 |
| Monagh Rd Bypass BT11 | 18 | D18 |
| Monarch Par BT12 | 19 | J17 |
| Monarch St BT12 | 19 | J17 |
| Moneyrea St BT6 | 21 | R17 |
| Montgomery Ct BT6 | 27 | S20 |
| Montgomery Rd BT6 | 27 | S20 |
| Montgomery St BT1 | 31 | E2 |
| Montreal St BT13 | 19 | H13 |
| Montrose St BT5 | 21 | R15 |
| Montrose S BT5 | 21 | R16 |
| Montrose Wk BT5 | | |
| *off Montrose St* | 21 | R15 |
| Moonstone St BT9 | 25 | J21 |
| Mooreland Cres BT11 | 25 | F21 |
| Mooreland Dr BT11 | 24 | E21 |
| Mooreland Pk BT11 | 24 | E21 |
| Moores Pl BT12 | 30 | B6 |
| Moorfield St BT5 | 21 | T16 |
| Moorgate St BT5 | 21 | T16 |
| Moor Pk Av BT10 | 24 | C23 |
| Moor Pk Dr BT10 | 24 | C23 |
| Moor Pk Gdns BT10 | 24 | C23 |
| Moor Pk Ms BT10 | 24 | C23 |
| Mornington BT7 | 26 | N22 |
| Mornington Ms BT7 | | |
| *off Mornington* | 26 | N22 |
| Mornington Pk BT7 | 26 | N22 |
| Mornington Pl BT7 | 26 | N22 |
| Morpeth St BT13 | | |
| *off Tyne St* | 19 | K14 |
| Moscow Rd BT3 | 16 | U10 |
| Moscow St BT13 | | |
| *off Shankill Rd* | 19 | K14 |
| Moss Rd, Hol. BT18 | 17 | AA12 |
| Mossvale St BT13 | 19 | H13 |
| Motelands BT4 | 17 | X12 |
| Mount, The BT5 | 21 | Q16 |
| Mount Aboo Pk BT10 | 24 | E24 |
| Mountainhill La BT14 | | |
| *off Mountainhill Rd* | 12 | E9 |
| Mountainhill Rd BT14 | 12 | E9 |
| Mountainhill Wk BT14 | | |
| *off Mountainhill Rd* | 12 | E9 |
| Mountainview Dr BT14 | 13 | G12 |
| Mountainview Gdns BT14 | 13 | G12 |
| Mountainview Par BT14 | 13 | G12 |
| Mountainview Pk BT14 | 13 | G12 |
| Mountainview Pl BT14 | 13 | G12 |
| Mount Alverno BT12 | 18 | D17 |
| Mount Carmel BT15 | 8 | L8 |
| Mount Charles BT7 | 20 | M18 |
| Mountcollyer Av BT15 | 14 | N12 |
| Mountcollyer Cl BT15 | | |
| *off Mountcollyer St* | 14 | M11 |
| Mountcollyer Rd BT15 | 14 | N12 |
| Mountcollyer St BT15 | 14 | M11 |
| Mount Coole Gdns BT14 | 8 | J8 |
| Mount Coole Pk BT14 | 8 | J8 |
| Mount Eden Ct BT13 | 13 | H12 |
| Mount Eden Pk BT9 | 25 | J23 |
| Mountforde Ct BT5 | | |
| *off Mountforde Dr* | 21 | Q15 |
| Mountforde Dr BT5 | 21 | Q15 |
| Mountforde Gdns BT5 | | |
| *off Mountforde Dr* | 21 | Q15 |
| Mountforde Pk BT5 | | |
| *off Mountforde Rd* | 21 | Q15 |
| Mountforde Rd BT5 | 21 | Q15 |
| Mountjoy St BT13 | 19 | J14 |
| Mount Merrion BT6 | 27 | R20 |
| Mount Merrion Av BT6 | 27 | R21 |
| Mount Merrion Cres BT6 | 27 | Q21 |
| Mount Merrion Dr BT6 | 27 | R21 |
| Mount Merrion Gdns BT6 | 27 | R21 |
| Mount Merrion Pk BT6 | 27 | Q22 |
| Mount Michael Dr BT8 | 27 | R24 |
| Mount Michael Gro BT8 | 27 | R24 |
| Mount Michael Pk BT8 | 27 | R24 |
| Mount Michael Vw BT8 | 27 | R24 |
| Mount Oriel BT8 | 27 | Q24 |
| Mount Pleasant BT9 | 26 | M20 |
| Mountpottinger Link BT5 | 21 | Q15 |
| Mountpottinger Rd BT5 | 21 | Q16 |
| Mount Prospect Pk BT9 | 19 | K18 |
| Mount St BT5 | 21 | Q16 |
| Mount St BT6 | 21 | Q16 |
| Mount St, New. BT36 | 9 | N4 |
| Mount St S BT6 | 21 | Q17 |
| Mount Vernon Ct BT15 | | |
| *off Mount Vernon La* | 9 | N8 |
| Mount Vernon Dr BT15 | 9 | N8 |
| Mount Vernon Gdns BT15 | 9 | M8 |
| Mount Vernon Gro BT15 | | |
| *off Mount Vernon Pk* | 9 | N8 |
| Mount Vernon La BT15 | 9 | M8 |
| Mount Vernon Pk BT15 | 9 | M8 |
| Mount Vernon Pas BT15 | 9 | N8 |
| Mount Vernon Rd BT15 | 9 | N8 |
| Mount Vernon Wk BT15 | 9 | N8 |
| Mountview Ct BT14 | 14 | K12 |
| Mountview St BT14 | 14 | K12 |
| Mourne Pk BT5 | | |
| *off Hornby St* | 21 | R15 |
| Mourne St BT5 | 21 | S16 |
| Mowhan St BT9 | 25 | J21 |
| Moyallon Gdns BT7 | 27 | P22 |
| Moyard Cres BT12 | 18 | E15 |
| Moyard Par BT12 | 18 | E16 |
| Moyard Pk BT12 | 18 | E15 |
| Moyne Pk BT5 | 29 | Z19 |
| Mulhouse Rd BT12 | 19 | K16 |
| Murray St BT1 | 30 | C3 |
| Musgrave Channel Rd BT3 | 21 | R13 |
| Musgrave Pk Ct BT9 | | |
| *off Stockmans La* | 25 | G22 |
| Musgrave St BT1 | | |
| *off Ann St* | 31 | F2 |
| Music Hall Ct BT1 | | |
| *off Music Hall La* | 31 | E3 |
| Music Hall La BT1 | 31 | E3 |
| My Ladys Mile, Hol. BT18 | 11 | Z6 |
| My Ladys Rd BT6 | 21 | Q17 |
| Myrtlefield Pk BT9 | 25 | H22 |

## N

|  | | |
|---|---|---|
| Nansen St BT12 | 19 | H17 |
| Napier St BT12 | | |
| *off Blondin St* | 20 | L18 |
| Naroon Pk BT11 | 24 | B20 |
| Nassau St BT13 | | |
| *off Beresford St* | 19 | K14 |
| Navan Grn BT11 | 24 | D20 |
| Navarra Pl, New. BT36 | 9 | M4 |
| Neills Hill Pk BT5 | 22 | V17 |
| Nelson Ct BT13 | 19 | J14 |
| Nelson Sq BT13 | | |
| *off Nelson Ct* | 19 | J14 |
| Nelson St BT15 | 20 | N14 |
| Nendrum Gdns BT5 | 21 | T17 |
| Netherleigh Pk BT4 | 23 | Y14 |
| Nevis Av BT4 | 21 | T15 |
| New Barnsley Cres BT12 | 18 | D16 |
| New Barnsley Dr BT12 | 18 | E16 |
| New Barnsley Gdns BT12 | 18 | E15 |
| New Barnsley Grn BT12 | 18 | E15 |
| New Barnsley Gro BT12 | 18 | E16 |
| New Barnsley Par BT12 | 18 | E16 |
| New Barnsley Pk BT12 | 18 | E16 |
| Newcastle Manor BT4 | 21 | R15 |
| Newcastle St BT4 | 21 | R15 |
| New Fm La BT14 | | |
| *off Leginn St* | 13 | F9 |
| Newforge Dale BT9 | 26 | K23 |
| New Forge Gra BT9 | 26 | K23 |
| Newforge La BT9 | 26 | K23 |
| Newington Av BT15 | 14 | L11 |
| Newington St BT15 | 14 | M11 |
| New Lo Gdns BT15 | 20 | M13 |
| New Lo Pl BT15 | | |
| *off New Lo Rd* | 20 | M13 |
| New Lo Rd BT15 | 14 | M12 |
| Newport Ct BT14 | 14 | K12 |
| Newry St BT6 | 21 | R17 |
| Newton Gdns, New. BT36 | 9 | N4 |
| Newton Pk BT8 | 27 | Q24 |
| Newtownards Rd BT4 | 21 | Q15 |
| Ninth St BT13 | 19 | K14 |
| Norbloom Gdns BT5 | 21 | T17 |
| Norbury St BT11 | 18 | F18 |
| Norfolk Dr BT11 | 18 | F18 |
| Norfolk Gdns BT11 | 18 | E18 |
| Norfolk Gro BT11 | 18 | E18 |
| Norfolk Par BT11 | 18 | E18 |
| Norfolk Rd BT11 | 18 | E18 |
| Norfolk Way BT11 | 18 | E18 |
| Norglen Cres BT11 | 18 | E17 |
| Norglen Dr BT11 | 18 | E18 |
| Norglen Gdns BT11 | 18 | D18 |
| Norglen Gro BT11 | 18 | E18 |
| Norglen Par BT11 | 18 | D17 |
| Norglen Rd BT11 | 18 | D18 |
| North Bk BT6 | 27 | R20 |
| North Boundary St BT13 | 20 | L14 |

|  | | |
|---|---|---|
| Northbrook Gdns BT9 | 25 | J19 |
| Northbrook St BT9 | 25 | J19 |
| North Circular Rd BT14 | 8 | K8 |
| North Circular Rd BT15 | 8 | K7 |
| North Cl, Hol. BT18 | 11 | Z7 |
| North Derby St BT15 | 14 | N11 |
| Northern Ireland Science | | |
| Pk BT3 | 15 | R12 |
| Northern Rd BT3 | 15 | P11 |
| Northfield Ri BT5 | 28 | W19 |
| North Gdns BT5 | 22 | U17 |
| North Grn BT11 | 24 | D20 |
| North Hill St BT15 | 20 | M13 |
| North Howard Ct BT13 | | |
| *off Fifth St* | 19 | K15 |
| North Howard Link | | |
| BT13 | 19 | K15 |
| North Howard St BT13 | 19 | K15 |
| North Howard Wk | | |
| BT13 | 19 | K14 |
| North King St BT13 | | |
| *off Gardiner St* | 20 | L14 |
| Northland Ct BT13 | | |
| *off Northland St* | 19 | J14 |
| Northlands Pk BT10 | 24 | D23 |
| Northland St BT13 | 19 | J14 |
| North Link BT11 | 24 | E20 |
| North Par BT7 | 27 | P20 |
| North Queen St BT15 | 20 | M13 |
| North Rd BT4 | 22 | U15 |
| North Rd BT5 | 22 | U17 |
| North Sperrin BT5 | 23 | AA17 |
| North St BT1 | 20 | M14 |
| North St Arc BT1 | | |
| *off North St* | 20 | M15 |
| Northumberland St | | |
| BT13 | 19 | K15 |
| Northwick Dr BT14 | 13 | H11 |
| Northwood Cres BT15 | 14 | N10 |
| Northwood Dr BT15 | 14 | N10 |
| Northwood Par BT15 | 14 | N10 |
| Northwood Rd BT15 | 14 | N10 |
| Norton Dr BT9 | 25 | J23 |
| Norwood Av BT4 | 22 | V15 |
| Norwood Ct BT4 | 22 | V14 |
| Norwood Cres BT4 | 22 | V14 |
| Norwood Dr BT4 | 22 | V15 |
| Norwood Gdns BT4 | 22 | W14 |
| Norwood Gro BT4 | 22 | V14 |
| Norwood La, Hol. BT18 | 11 | Z7 |
| Norwood Pk BT4 | 22 | W14 |
| Norwood St BT12 | | |
| *off Wellwood St* | 30 | C5 |
| Notting Hill BT9 | 26 | K21 |
| Notting Hill Ct BT9 | 26 | L21 |
| Notting Hill Manor BT9 | 26 | K21 |
| Nubia St BT12 | 19 | J18 |
| Nun's Wk, Hol. BT18 | 11 | AA8 |

**O**

|  | | |
|---|---|---|
| Oakdale St BT5 | 21 | S16 |
| Oakdene Dr BT4 | 21 | T14 |
| Oakdene Par BT4 | 21 | T14 |
| Oakfield St BT14 | 13 | J12 |
| Oakhill BT5 | 28 | V21 |
| Oakhurst Av BT10 | 24 | C24 |
| Oakland Av BT4 | 22 | U16 |
| Oakleigh Pk BT6 | 21 | Q18 |
| Oakley Av, Hol. BT18 | 11 | Z8 |
| Oakley St BT14 | 13 | F10 |
| Oakman St BT12 | 19 | H16 |
| Oakmount Dr BT15 | 14 | N9 |
| Oak St BT7 | | |
| *off Elm St* | 30 | D6 |
| Oak Way BT7 | 30 | D6 |
| Oakwood Ct BT9 | 25 | J23 |
| Oakwood Gro BT9 | 25 | J23 |
| Oakwood Ms BT9 | 25 | J23 |
| Oakwood Pk BT9 | 25 | J23 |
| Oban St BT12 | 20 | L18 |
| Oberon St BT4 | 27 | R19 |
| Oceanic Av BT15 | 14 | L11 |
| O'Dempsey St BT15 | 14 | N10 |
| Odessa St BT13 | 19 | J15 |
| Ogilvie St BT6 | 21 | R18 |
| Ohio St BT13 | 19 | H13 |
| Old Bakers Ct BT6 | 21 | Q18 |
| Old Brewery La BT11 | 24 | D19 |
| Old Cavehill Rd BT15 | 8 | K7 |
| Old Channel Rd BT3 | 20 | P14 |
| Old Dundonald Rd | | |
| (Dundonald) BT16 | 23 | BB17 |
| Old Golf Course Rd | | |
| (Dunmurry) BT17 | 24 | B24 |
| Old Holywood Rd BT4 | 22 | X13 |
| Old Holywood Rd, Hol. | | |
| BT18 | 17 | Z9 |
| Old Mill Rd BT14 | 12 | E9 |
| Old Mill Way BT14 | | |
| *off Old Mill Rd* | 13 | F9 |
| Oldpark Av BT14 | 14 | K11 |
| Oldpark Rd BT14 | 13 | H9 |
| Oldpark Sq BT14 | | |
| *off Ardoyne Av* | 13 | J12 |
| Oldpark Ter BT14 | 13 | J10 |
| Old Quay Ct, Hol. BT18 | 11 | BB5 |
| Old Quay Rd, Hol. | | |
| BT18 | 11 | BB4 |
| Old Westland Rd BT14 | 14 | K9 |
| Olive St BT13 | 19 | H13 |
| Olympia Dr BT12 | 25 | J19 |
| Olympia Par BT12 | 25 | J19 |
| Olympia St BT12 | 25 | J19 |
| Omeath St BT6 | 21 | R18 |
| O'Neills Pl, Hol. BT18 | | |
| *off Church Vw* | 11 | AA6 |
| O'Neill St BT13 | 19 | J16 |
| Onslow Gdns BT6 | 27 | R20 |
| Onslow Par BT6 | 27 | R20 |
| Onslow Pk BT6 | 27 | R20 |
| Ophir Gdns BT15 | 8 | K8 |
| Orangefield Av BT5 | 22 | U17 |
| Orangefield Cres BT6 | 27 | S19 |
| Orangefield Dr BT5 | 22 | U17 |
| Orangefield Dr S BT5 | 22 | U17 |
| Orangefield Gdns BT5 | 22 | U17 |
| Orangefield Grn BT5 | 22 | U17 |
| Orangefield Gro BT5 | 22 | U17 |
| Orangefield La BT5 | 22 | U17 |
| Orangefield Par BT5 | 22 | U17 |
| Orangefield Pk BT5 | 22 | U18 |
| Orangefield Rd BT5 | 22 | U17 |
| Oranmore Dr BT11 | 24 | B23 |
| Oranmore St BT13 | 19 | J15 |
| Orby Chase BT5 | 21 | T17 |
| Orby Ct BT5 | 21 | T18 |
| Orby Dr BT5 | 21 | T18 |
| Orby Gdns BT5 | 21 | S18 |
| Orby Gra BT5 | 21 | T18 |
| Orby Grn BT5 | 21 | S18 |
| Orby Gro BT5 | 21 | T18 |
| Orby Link BT5 | 21 | S18 |
| Orby Ms BT5 | 21 | T18 |
| Orby Mills BT5 | 21 | S18 |
| Orby Par BT5 | 21 | T18 |
| Orby Pk BT5 | 28 | T19 |
| Orby Pl BT5 | 21 | S18 |
| Orby Rd BT5 | 21 | S18 |
| Orby St BT5 | 28 | U19 |
| Orchard Cl BT5 | 23 | Y18 |
| Orchard Ct, Hol. BT18 | 17 | X11 |
| Orchard La BT14 | 22 | W14 |
| Orchard St BT15 | 14 | N12 |
| Orchardvale BT18 | 28 | T21 |
| Orchardville Av BT10 | 24 | E23 |
| Orchardville Cres BT10 | 24 | E23 |
| Orchardville Gdns | | |
| BT10 | 24 | E23 |
| Oregon Gdns BT13 | 19 | J13 |
| Orient Gdns BT14 | 14 | L11 |
| Orkney St BT13 | 19 | J14 |
| Ormeau Av BT2 | 30 | D5 |
| Ormeau Br BT7 | 26 | N19 |
| Ormeau Embk BT6 | 31 | G6 |
| Ormeau Embk BT7 | 27 | P19 |
| Ormeau Rd BT7 | 31 | E6 |
| Ormeau St BT7 | 31 | E6 |
| Ormiston Cres BT4 | 22 | W16 |
| Ormiston Dr BT4 | 22 | X16 |
| Ormiston Gdns BT5 | 22 | W16 |
| Ormiston Par BT4 | 22 | X16 |
| Ormiston Pk BT4 | 22 | X16 |
| Ormiston Sq BT4 | 22 | W15 |
| Ormonde Av BT10 | 24 | E24 |
| Ormonde Cres BT6 | 21 | S18 |
| Ormonde Gdns BT6 | 21 | S18 |
| Ormonde Pk BT10 | 24 | D24 |
| Ormond Pl BT12 | | |
| *off Roumania Ri* | 19 | K15 |
| Orpen Av BT10 | 24 | E24 |
| Orpen Dr BT10 | 24 | E24 |
| Orpen Pk BT10 | 24 | E24 |
| Orpen Rd BT10 | 24 | E24 |
| Osborne Dr BT9 | 25 | J21 |
| Osborne Gdns BT9 | 25 | J22 |
| Osborne Pk BT9 | 25 | H21 |
| Osborne Pl BT9 | 25 | H21 |
| Osman St BT12 | 19 | K16 |
| Oswald Pk BT12 | 30 | A6 |
| Ottawa St BT13 | 19 | H13 |
| Oval Ct BT4 | | |
| *off Oval St* | 21 | S15 |
| Oval St BT4 | 21 | S15 |
| Owenvale Ms BT13 | 18 | F15 |
| Owenvarragh Gdns BT11 | | |
| *off Owenvarragh Pk* | 25 | F21 |
| Owenvarragh Pk BT11 | 24 | E21 |
| Oxford St BT1 | 31 | F2 |

**P**

|  | | |
|---|---|---|
| Pacific Av BT15 | 14 | L11 |
| Pakenham Ms BT7 | | |
| *off Pakenham St* | 30 | D6 |
| Pakenham St BT7 | 30 | C6 |
| Palace Gdns BT15 | 14 | L9 |
| Palace Gro, Hol. BT18 | 17 | Z9 |
| Palestine St BT7 | 26 | N19 |
| Palmer Ct BT13 | | |
| *off Palmer St* | 13 | H12 |
| Palmerston Pk BT4 | 22 | U13 |
| Palmerston Rd BT4 | 22 | U14 |
| Palmer St BT13 | 19 | H13 |
| Pandora St BT12 | 19 | K18 |
| Pansy St BT4 | 21 | S15 |
| Panton St BT12 | | |
| *off Ross Rd* | 19 | K15 |
| Paris St BT13 | 19 | K14 |
| Park Av BT4 | 21 | T14 |
| Park Av, Hol. BT18 | 11 | AA6 |
| Park Cen BT12 | 19 | H17 |
| Park Dr, Hol. BT18 | 11 | Z6 |
| Parkend St BT15 | 14 | M11 |
| Parker St BT5 | 21 | R15 |
| Parkgate Av BT4 | 21 | T15 |
| Parkgate Cres BT4 | 21 | S15 |
| Parkgate Dr BT4 | 21 | S15 |
| Parkgate Gdns BT4 | 21 | T15 |
| Parkgate Par BT4 | 21 | T15 |
| Park Gra BT4 | | |
| *off Park Av* | 21 | T15 |
| Park La BT9 | 26 | L19 |
| Parkmore St BT7 | 27 | P20 |
| Parkmount Ct BT15 | 14 | N11 |
| Parkmount Gdns BT15 | 9 | N6 |
| Parkmount La BT15 | 9 | N6 |
| Parkmount Pas BT15 | 9 | N6 |
| Parkmount Pl BT15 | 9 | N6 |
| Parkmount Rd BT15 | 9 | M7 |
| Parkmount St BT15 | 14 | N11 |
| Parkmount Ter BT15 | 9 | N6 |
| Parkmount Way BT15 | 9 | N6 |
| Park Par BT6 | 21 | Q17 |
| Park Pl BT6 | 21 | Q18 |
| Park Rd BT7 | 27 | P20 |
| Park Royal Balmoral BT9 | | |
| *off Lisburn Rd* | 25 | G22 |
| Parkside Gdns BT15 | 14 | M11 |
| Parkview St BT14 | | |
| *off Glenview St* | 14 | K12 |
| Parkville Ct BT15 | 14 | L9 |
| Parkvue Manor BT5 | 23 | Y18 |
| Pasadena Gdns BT5 | 22 | W16 |
| Patterson's Pl BT1 | | |
| *off Upper Arthur St* | 31 | E3 |
| Pattons La, Hol. BT18 | | |
| *off Church Vw* | 11 | Z6 |
| Paulett Av BT5 | | |
| *off Albertbridge Rd* | 21 | R16 |
| Pavilions Office Pk, Hol. | | |
| BT18 | 11 | Y6 |
| Paxton St BT5 | 21 | R16 |
| Pearl Ct BT6 | 21 | R17 |
| Pearl St BT6 | 21 | R17 |
| Pembridge Ct BT4 | 22 | W15 |
| Pembridge Ms BT5 | 22 | V17 |
| Pembroke St BT12 | 19 | K18 |
| Penge Gdns BT9 | 26 | M21 |
| Penrose St BT7 | 20 | N18 |
| Pepperhill St BT13 | | |
| *off Stanhope Dr* | 20 | M14 |
| Percy Pl BT13 | 20 | L14 |
| Percy St BT13 | 19 | K15 |
| Pernau St BT13 | 19 | K14 |
| Perry Ct BT5 | 21 | Q16 |
| Peters Hill BT13 | 20 | L14 |
| Phennick Dr BT10 | 25 | F24 |
| Picardy Av BT6 | 27 | S20 |
| Pilot Pl BT1 | | |
| *off Pilot St* | 20 | P13 |
| Pilot St BT1 | 20 | P13 |
| Pims Av BT13 | 21 | T15 |
| Pim St BT15 | 20 | M13 |
| Pine Crest, Hol. BT18 | 11 | AA7 |
| Pine Gro, Hol. BT18 | | |
| *off Loughview Av* | 11 | Z8 |
| Pine St BT7 | 31 | E6 |
| Pine Way BT7 | 31 | E6 |
| Piney Hills BT9 | 26 | K24 |
| Piney La BT9 | 26 | K24 |
| Piney Pk BT9 | 26 | K24 |
| Piney Wk BT9 | 26 | K24 |
| Piney Way BT9 | 26 | K24 |
| Pinkerton Wk BT15 | 20 | M13 |
| Pirrie Pk Gdns BT6 | 27 | Q19 |
| Pirrie Rd BT4 | 22 | W15 |
| Pitt Pl BT1 | 21 | Q15 |
| Pittsburg St BT15 | 14 | N10 |
| Plas Merdyn, Hol. BT18 | 11 | BB7 |
| Plateau, The BT9 | 26 | K24 |
| Plevna Pk BT12 | | |
| *off Osman St* | 19 | K16 |
| Plunkett Ct BT13 | | |
| *off Plunkett St* | 20 | M14 |
| Plunkett St BT13 | 20 | M14 |
| Pollard Cl BT12 | 19 | H15 |
| Pollard St BT12 | 19 | H15 |
| Pollock Rd BT3 | 15 | P12 |
| Pommern Par BT6 | 27 | S19 |
| Pomona Av BT4 | 21 | T15 |
| Ponsonby Av BT15 | 14 | L12 |
| Portallo St BT6 | 21 | R18 |
| Porter Pk BT10 | 24 | E24 |
| Portland Pl BT15 | 20 | M14 |
| Portnamona Ct BT11 | 24 | D19 |
| Posnett Ct BT7 | 30 | D6 |
| Posnett St BT7 | 30 | C6 |
| Pottingers Ct BT1 | | |
| *off Ann St* | 31 | E2 |
| Pottingers Entry BT1 | | |
| *off High St* | 31 | E2 |
| Pottinger St BT5 | 21 | R17 |
| Powerscourt St BT13 | 20 | N18 |
| Premier Dr BT15 | 14 | M9 |
| Premier Gro BT15 | 14 | M10 |
| Prestwick Dr BT14 | 13 | H9 |
| Prestwick Pk BT14 | 13 | H9 |
| Pretoria St BT9 | 26 | M19 |
| Primrose St BT7 | 27 | P20 |
| Primrose St BT14 | 13 | F10 |
| Prince Andrew Gdns | | |
| BT12 | 19 | K17 |
| Prince Andrew Pk | | |
| BT12 | 19 | K17 |
| Prince Edward Dr BT9 | 26 | M22 |
| Prince Edward Gdns | | |
| BT9 | 26 | M22 |
| Prince Edward Pk BT9 | 26 | M21 |
| Prince of Wales Av BT4 | 23 | Z16 |
| Prince Regent Rd BT5 | 28 | V20 |
| Princes Ct BT1 | | |
| *off Queens Sq* | 31 | F1 |
| Princes Dock St BT1 | 20 | P13 |
| Princes St BT1 | | |
| *off Queens Sq* | 31 | F1 |
| Princes St Ct BT1 | | |
| *off Queens Sq* | 31 | F1 |
| Prior's Lea, Hol. BT18 | | |
| *off Firmount Cres* | 17 | Z9 |
| Priory End, Hol. BT18 | 11 | Z7 |
| Priory Gdns BT10 | 25 | F23 |
| Priory Pk BT10 | 25 | F23 |

| | | | |
|---|---|---|---|
| Priory Pk, Hol. BT18 | 11 | AA5 | |
| Prospect Pk BT14 | 13 | J12 | |
| Prospect Ter, Hol. BT18 | | | |
| *off Kinnegar Rd* | 11 | Y6 | |
| Purdys La BT8 | 27 | Q24 | |

**Q**

| | | |
|---|---|---|
| Quadrant Pl BT12 | 30 | A2 |
| Quarry Hill BT5 | 28 | W21 |
| Quarry Rd BT4 | 17 | X12 |
| Queen Elizabeth Br | | |
| BT1 | 31 | F1 |
| Queen Elizabeth Br | | |
| BT3 | 31 | F1 |
| Queens Arc BT1 | 30 | D2 |
| Queensberry Pk BT6 | 27 | Q22 |
| Queen's Br BT1 | 31 | F2 |
| Queen's Br BT4 | 31 | G1 |
| Queensland St BT13 | 19 | K13 |
| Queens Par BT15 | 20 | M13 |
| Queens Quay BT3 | 31 | G1 |
| Queens Quay Rd BT3 | 20 | P14 |
| Queens Rd BT3 | 20 | P14 |
| Queens Sq BT1 | 31 | F1 |
| Queen St BT1 | 30 | C3 |
| Queen Victoria Gdns | | |
| BT15 | 14 | M10 |
| Queen Victoria St BT5 | 21 | T16 |
| Quinton St BT5 | 21 | S17 |
| Quinville, Hol. BT18 | | |
| *off Spencer St* | 11 | AA6 |

**R**

| | | |
|---|---|---|
| Raby St BT7 | 27 | P20 |
| Radnor St BT6 | 21 | Q17 |
| Rainey Way BT7 | | |
| *off Lindsay St* | 30 | D5 |
| Raleigh St BT13 | 19 | K13 |
| Ramoan Dr BT11 | 24 | C20 |
| Ramoan Gdns BT11 | 24 | C20 |
| Randal Pk BT9 | 25 | J21 |
| Ranelagh St BT6 | 21 | R18 |
| Ranfurly Dr BT4 | 22 | U15 |
| Raphael St BT7 | 31 | E5 |
| Ratcliffe St BT7 | 30 | C6 |
| Rathbone St BT2 | | |
| *off Little May St* | 31 | E3 |
| Rathcool St BT9 | 25 | J20 |
| Rathdrum St BT9 | 25 | J20 |
| Rathgar St BT9 | 25 | J20 |
| Rathlin St BT13 | 19 | H13 |
| Rath Mor BT11 | 24 | C22 |
| Rathmore St BT6 | 21 | Q17 |
| Ravenhill Av BT6 | 21 | Q18 |
| Ravenhill Ct BT6 | 21 | Q18 |
| Ravenhill Cres BT6 | 21 | Q18 |
| Ravenhill Gdns BT6 | 21 | Q19 |
| Ravenhill Ms BT6 | 21 | Q18 |
| Ravenhill Par BT6 | 21 | R18 |
| Ravenhill Pk BT6 | 27 | Q20 |
| Ravenhill Pk Gdns BT6 | 27 | Q20 |
| Ravenhill Reach BT6 | 31 | H5 |
| Ravenhill Reach Ct BT6 | | |
| *off Ravenhill Reach* | 31 | H5 |
| Ravenhill Reach Ms | | |
| BT6 | 31 | H5 |
| Ravenhill Rd BT6 | 27 | P21 |
| Ravenhill St BT6 | 21 | Q17 |
| Ravenscroft Av BT5 | 21 | T16 |
| Ravenscroft St BT5 | 21 | T16 |
| Ravensdale Ct BT5 | 21 | R17 |
| Ravensdale Cres BT5 | 21 | R17 |
| Ravensdale St BT5 | 21 | R17 |
| Ravensdene Cres BT6 | 27 | Q19 |
| Ravensdene Ms BT6 | 27 | Q19 |
| Ravensdene Pk BT6 | 27 | Q19 |
| Ravensdene Pk Gdns | | |
| BT6 | 27 | Q20 |
| Ravenswood Cres BT5 | 29 | X20 |
| Ravenswood Pk BT5 | 28 | W20 |
| Redburn Sq, Hol. BT18 | 11 | Z6 |
| Redcar St BT6 | 21 | R18 |
| Redcliffe Dr BT4 | 21 | S15 |
| Redcliffe Par BT4 | 21 | S15 |
| Redcliffe St BT4 | 21 | S15 |
| Regent St BT13 | 20 | L13 |
| Regent's Wd BT9 | 25 | J24 |
| Reid St BT6 | 27 | R19 |

| | | |
|---|---|---|
| Renfrew Ho BT12 | | |
| *off Rowland Way* | 30 | B5 |
| Renfrew Wk BT12 | | |
| *off Rowland Way* | 30 | B5 |
| Renwick St BT12 | 30 | C6 |
| Riada Cl BT4 | 21 | R15 |
| Ribble St BT4 | 21 | S15 |
| Richardson Ct BT6 | | |
| *off Richardson St* | 21 | Q17 |
| Richardson St BT6 | 21 | Q17 |
| Richdale Dr, Hol. BT18 | 11 | BB4 |
| Richhill Cres BT5 | 22 | W17 |
| Richhill Pk BT5 | 22 | W18 |
| Richmond Av, Hol. | | |
| BT18 | 17 | X10 |
| Richmond Cl, Hol. | | |
| BT18 | 17 | X10 |
| Richmond Ct, Hol. | | |
| BT18 | 17 | X10 |
| Richmond Grn, Hol. | | |
| BT18 | 17 | X11 |
| Richmond Hts, Hol. | | |
| BT18 | 17 | X10 |
| Richmond Ms BT10 | 25 | F23 |
| Richmond Pk BT9 | 26 | L22 |
| Richmond Pk BT10 | 25 | F23 |
| Richmond Sq BT15 | 14 | L10 |
| Richview St BT12 | 19 | K17 |
| Ridgeway St BT9 | 26 | M20 |
| Riga St BT13 | 19 | J14 |
| Rigby Cl BT15 | 14 | L9 |
| Ringford Cres BT11 | 24 | B22 |
| Ringford Pk BT11 | | |
| *off Ringford Cres* | 24 | B22 |
| Rinnalea Cl BT11 | 24 | B21 |
| Rinnalea Gdns BT11 | 24 | B21 |
| Rinnalea Gro BT11 | 24 | B22 |
| Rinnalea Wk BT11 | | |
| *off Rinnalea Way* | 24 | B21 |
| Rinnalea Way BT11 | 24 | B21 |
| Ritchie St BT15 | 14 | N11 |
| River Cl BT11 | 24 | C23 |
| Riverdale Cl BT11 | 24 | E21 |
| Riverdale Gdns BT11 | 24 | D21 |
| Riverdale Pk Av BT11 | 24 | D21 |
| Riverdale Pk Dr BT11 | 24 | D21 |
| Riverdale Pk E BT11 | 24 | E21 |
| Riverdale Pk N BT11 | 24 | D21 |
| Riverdale Pk S BT11 | 24 | D22 |
| Riverdale Pk W BT11 | 24 | D21 |
| Riverdale Pl BT11 | 24 | E21 |
| Riversdale St BT13 | | |
| *off North* | | |
| *Boundary St* | 20 | L14 |
| Riverside Sq BT12 | | |
| *off Roden Way* | 19 | K16 |
| Riverside Vw BT7 | 26 | N22 |
| Riverside Way BT12 | 19 | K17 |
| River Ter BT7 | 31 | F6 |
| Riverview St BT9 | 26 | M20 |
| Robina St BT15 | 14 | M12 |
| Robina St BT15 | 14 | M11 |
| Rochester Av BT6 | 27 | S21 |
| Rochester Ct BT6 | | |
| *off Clonduff Dr* | 28 | U20 |
| Rochester Dr BT6 | 27 | S21 |
| Rochester Rd BT6 | 28 | T21 |
| Rochester St BT6 | 21 | Q17 |
| Rockdale St BT12 | 19 | G17 |
| Rock Gro BT12 | | |
| *off Glenalina Cres* | 18 | E17 |
| Rockland St BT12 | 19 | J17 |
| Rockmore Rd BT12 | 19 | G17 |
| Rockmount St BT12 | 19 | G17 |
| Rockview St BT12 | 19 | J18 |
| Rockville Cl BT4 | 22 | V13 |
| Rockville Ms BT4 | 22 | V13 |
| Rockville St BT12 | 19 | G17 |
| Rocky Rd BT5 | 29 | Z21 |
| Rocky Rd BT6 | 27 | S22 |
| Rocky Rd BT8 | 28 | T22 |
| Roddens Cres BT5 | 28 | V20 |
| Roddens Gdns BT5 | 28 | V20 |
| Roddens Pk BT5 | 28 | V20 |
| Roden Pas BT12 | 19 | K16 |
| Roden Sq BT12 | | |
| *off Roden Way* | 19 | K16 |
| Roden St BT12 | 19 | K17 |

| | | |
|---|---|---|
| Roden Way BT12 | 19 | K16 |
| Rodney Dr BT12 | 19 | H18 |
| Rodney Par BT12 | 19 | H18 |
| Roosevelt Ri BT12 | 19 | K17 |
| Roosevelt Sq BT12 | 19 | K17 |
| Roosevelt St BT12 | 19 | K17 |
| Rosapenna Ct BT14 | 14 | K12 |
| *off Rosapenna St* | 14 | K12 |
| Rosapenna Dr BT14 | 14 | K12 |
| Rosapenna Par BT14 | 14 | K11 |
| Rosapenna St BT14 | 14 | K12 |
| Rosapenna Wk BT14 | 14 | K12 |
| Rosebank Ct BT14 | | |
| *off Glenview St* | 14 | K12 |
| Rosebank St BT13 | | |
| *off Ohio St* | 19 | J13 |
| Rosebery Gdns BT6 | 21 | R18 |
| Rosebery Rd BT6 | 21 | Q17 |
| Rosebery St BT5 | 21 | T16 |
| Roseland Pl BT12 | 30 | A6 |
| Roseleigh St BT14 | 14 | K12 |
| Rosemary Pk BT9 | 25 | J24 |
| Rosemary St BT1 | 30 | D1 |
| Rosemount Av BT5 | 23 | AA16 |
| Rosemount Gdns BT15 | 14 | L10 |
| Rosemount Pk BT5 | 28 | V21 |
| Rosepark BT5 | 23 | AA16 |
| Rosepark Cen BT5 | 23 | AA16 |
| Rosepark E BT5 | 23 | AA16 |
| Rosepark Meadows BT5 | | |
| *off Rosepark* | 23 | AA17 |
| Rosepark S BT5 | 23 | AA16 |
| Rosepark W BT5 | 23 | AA17 |
| Rosetta Av BT7 | 27 | P21 |
| Rosetta Dr BT7 | 27 | P22 |
| Rosetta Par BT7 | 27 | P22 |
| Rosetta Pk BT6 | 27 | Q21 |
| Rosetta Rd BT6 | 27 | Q21 |
| Rosetta Rd E BT6 | 27 | R22 |
| Rosetta Way BT6 | 27 | P21 |
| Rosevale St BT14 | 14 | K12 |
| Rosewood Ct BT14 | 14 | K12 |
| Rosewood Pk BT6 | 28 | V20 |
| Rosewood St BT14 | 19 | K13 |
| Rosgoill Dr BT11 | 24 | B21 |
| Rosgoill Gdns BT11 | 24 | B21 |
| Rosgoill Pk BT11 | 24 | C21 |
| Roslin Gdns BT5 | 23 | AA18 |
| Roslyn St BT6 | 21 | Q17 |
| Rosscoole Pk BT14 | 8 | J7 |
| Ross Cotts BT12 | | |
| *off Ross St* | 19 | K15 |
| Ross Ct BT12 | 19 | K15 |
| Ross Mill Av BT13 | 19 | J15 |
| Rossmore Av BT7 | 27 | P21 |
| Rossmore Dr BT7 | 27 | P21 |
| Rossmore Pk BT7 | 27 | P21 |
| Rossnareen Av BT11 | 24 | C20 |
| Rossnareen Ct BT11 | 24 | C20 |
| Rossnareen Pk BT11 | 24 | C20 |
| Rossnareen Rd BT11 | 24 | C20 |
| Ross Ri BT12 | | |
| *off Ross Rd* | 19 | K15 |
| Ross Rd BT12 | 19 | K15 |
| Ross St BT12 | 19 | K15 |
| Rothsay Sq BT14 | | |
| *off Ardilea St* | 13 | J12 |
| Rothsay St BT14 | | |
| *off Glenpark St* | 13 | J12 |
| Rotterdam Ct BT5 | 31 | G2 |
| Rotterdam St BT5 | 31 | G2 |
| Roumania Ri BT12 | 19 | K15 |
| Roundhill St BT5 | 21 | R16 |
| Rowland Way BT12 | 30 | B5 |
| Royal Av BT1 | 30 | D1 |
| Rugby Av BT7 | 20 | N18 |
| Rugby Ct BT7 | 26 | N19 |
| Rugby Ms BT7 | | |
| *off Rugby St* | 26 | M19 |
| Rugby Par BT7 | 26 | N19 |
| Rugby Rd BT7 | 20 | M18 |
| Rugby St BT7 | 26 | N19 |
| Rumford St BT13 | 19 | K14 |
| Runnymede Dr BT12 | 25 | J19 |
| Runnymede Par BT12 | 25 | J19 |
| Rushfield Av BT7 | 26 | N21 |
| Rusholme St BT13 | 19 | K13 |

| | | |
|---|---|---|
| Russell Pk BT5 | 29 | AA19 |
| Russell Pl BT2 | 31 | E4 |
| Russell St BT2 | 31 | E4 |
| Rutherford St BT13 | | |
| *off Hopewell Cres* | 20 | L14 |
| Rutherglen St BT13 | 13 | G12 |
| Rutland St BT7 | 20 | N18 |
| Rydalmere St BT12 | 19 | J17 |

**S**

| | | |
|---|---|---|
| Sackville Ct BT13 | 30 | B1 |
| Sagimor Gdns BT5 | 21 | T16 |
| St. Agnes Dr BT11 | 24 | D21 |
| St. Agnes Pl BT11 | 24 | D21 |
| St. Albans Gdns BT9 | 26 | M20 |
| St. Andrews Sq E BT12 | | |
| *off Hope St* | 30 | C4 |
| St. Andrews Sq N BT12 | | |
| *off Hope St* | 30 | B4 |
| St. Andrews Sq W BT12 | | |
| *off Hope St* | 30 | B4 |
| St. Annes Cl BT10 | 24 | D24 |
| St. Annes Cres BT10 | 24 | D24 |
| St. Annes La BT10 | 24 | D24 |
| St. Aubyn St BT15 | 14 | N10 |
| St. Columbans Ct BT14 | | |
| *off Glenview St* | 14 | K12 |
| Saintfield Rd BT8 | 27 | P22 |
| St. Gall's Av BT13 | 19 | J15 |
| St. Gemmas Ct BT14 | 13 | J12 |
| St. Georges Gdns BT12 | | |
| *off Albion St* | 30 | C6 |
| St. Georges Harbour | | |
| BT7 | 31 | H4 |
| St. George's Mkt BT1 | 31 | F3 |
| St. Gerards Manor | | |
| BT12 | 18 | D16 |
| St. Helens Ct, Hol. | | |
| BT18 | 11 | Z6 |
| St. Ives Gdns BT9 | 26 | M20 |
| St. James Av BT13 | | |
| *off Highcairn Dr* | 18 | F14 |
| St. James Ms BT14 | 20 | L13 |
| St. James's Av BT12 | 19 | H17 |
| St. James's Cres BT12 | 19 | H18 |
| St. James's Dr BT12 | 19 | G18 |
| St. James's Gdns BT12 | 19 | H18 |
| St. James's Par BT12 | 19 | G18 |
| St. James's Pk BT12 | 19 | H18 |
| St. James's Pl BT12 | 19 | H18 |
| St. James's Rd BT12 | 19 | G18 |
| St. James's St BT14 | 20 | L13 |
| St. Johns Av BT7 | 27 | P22 |
| St. Johns Ct BT7 | | |
| *off St. Johns Pk* | 27 | P22 |
| St. Johns Pk BT7 | 27 | P22 |
| St. John's Pl BT7 | 27 | P22 |
| St. Johns Sq BT7 | 27 | P22 |
| St. Judes Av BT7 | 27 | P21 |
| St. Judes Cres BT7 | 27 | P22 |
| St. Judes Par BT7 | 27 | P20 |
| St. Judes Sq BT7 | 27 | P20 |
| St. Katharine Rd BT12 | 19 | H18 |
| St. Kilda Ct BT6 | 31 | H5 |
| St. Kilda St BT6 | 31 | H5 |
| St. Leonards Cres BT4 | | |
| *off St. Leonards St* | 21 | R15 |
| St. Leonards St BT4 | 21 | R15 |
| St. Lukes Cl BT13 | | |
| *off Carlow St* | 19 | K14 |
| St. Lukes Wk BT13 | | |
| *off Carlow St* | 19 | K15 |
| St. Marys Ct BT13 | | |
| *off Silvio St* | 19 | K13 |
| St. Marys Gdns BT12 | 19 | G16 |
| St. Matthew's Ct BT5 | | |
| *off Seaforde St* | 21 | Q15 |
| St. Meryl Pk BT11 | 24 | E19 |
| St. Patrick's Wk BT4 | | |
| *off Newtownards Rd* | 21 | R15 |
| St. Pauls Fold BT15 | | |
| *off Canning St* | 14 | N12 |
| St. Pauls St BT15 | 14 | N12 |
| St. Peters Cl BT12 | | |
| *off Albert St* | 19 | K15 |
| St. Peters Ct BT12 | 19 | K15 |
| St. Peter's Pl BT12 | 19 | K15 |
| *off Ardmoulin St* | 19 | K15 |

St. Peters Sq E BT12  
*off Ardmoulin St* 19 K15  
St. Peters Sq N BT12  
*off Ardmoulin St* 19 K15  
St. Peters Sq S BT12  
*off Ardmoulin St* 19 K15  
St. Stephens Ct BT13  
*off Brown Sq* 20 L14  
St. Vincent St BT15 14 N10  
Saleen Pk, Hol. BT18  
*off Priory Pk* 11 AA5  
Salisbury Ct BT7 8 L8  
Salisbury Ct BT7 30 D6  
Salisbury Gdns BT15 8 L8  
Salisbury La BT7  
*off Salisbury St* 30 D5  
Salisbury St BT7 30 C5  
Samuel St BT1 20 M14  
Sancroft St BT13 19 K13  
Sandbrook Gdns BT4 21 T14  
Sandbrook Gro BT4 21 T14  
Sandbrook Pk BT4 21 T14  
Sandford Av BT5 22 U16  
Sandhill Dr BT5 22 U17  
Sandhill Gdns BT5 22 V17  
Sandhill Grn BT5  
*off Sandhill Pk* 22 V17  
Sandhill Par BT5 22 V17  
Sandhill Pk BT5 22 U17  
Sandhurst Ct BT9  
*off Colenso Par* 26 M19  
Sandhurst Dr BT9 26 M20  
Sandhurst Gdns BT9 26 M20  
Sandhurst Rd BT7 20 N18  
Sandown Dr BT5 22 V16  
Sandown Pk BT5 22 W17  
Sandown Pk S BT5 22 V17  
Sandown Rd BT5 22 V17  
Sandringham Ms BT5 22 X16  
Sandringham St BT9 26 K19  
Sandymount St BT9 26 M20  
Sandy Row BT12 30 B5  
Sans Souci La BT9 26 L20  
Sans Souci Pk BT9 26 L20  
Santiago St BT13  
*off Madras St* 19 J13  
Sarajac Cres BT14 8 J8  
Sark St BT4 21 R15  
Saul St BT5  
*off Vulcan St* 21 Q15  
Saunders Cl BT4 21 R15  
Saunderson Ct BT14  
*off Glenpark St* 13 J12  
Sawel Hill BT11 24 D21  
Schomberg Av BT4 22 X14  
Schomberg Dr BT12 30 B6  
Schomberg Lo BT4 22 X14  
Schomberg Pk BT4 22 X14  
Schomberg St BT12 30 B6  
School Ct BT4 17 X11  
School Rd BT8 27 Q24  
Scotch Row BT4  
*off Newtownards Rd* 21 R15  
Scotts Ct BT4 21 T16  
Scotts Ms BT4 21 T16  
Scrabo St BT5 31 G1  
Seabank Par BT15 14 N9  
Seabourne Par BT15 14 M9  
Seaforde Ct BT5  
*off Seaforde St* 21 Q15  
Seaforde Gdns BT5  
*off Seaforde St* 21 Q15  
Seaforde St BT5 21 Q15  
Seagrove Par BT15 14 N9  
Seagrove Pl BT15  
*off Premier Dr* 14 M9  
Seaholm Par BT15 14 N9  
Sealands Par BT15 14 N9  
Seal Rd BT3 15 R9  
Seamount BT15 14 N9  
Seamount Par BT15 14 N9  
Seapark Av, Hol. BT18 11 AA5  
Seapark Ct, Hol. BT18 11 AA5  
Seapark Dr BT15 14 N9  
Seapark Gro, Hol. BT18 11 BB5  
Seapark Ms, Hol. BT18 11 BB5  
Seapark Rd, Hol. BT18 11 AA4  
Seapark Ter, Hol. BT18 11 AA5  

Seascape Par BT15 14 M9  
Seaview Cl BT15 14 N11  
Seaview Dr BT15 14 M9  
Seaview Gdns BT15 14 N9  
Seaview St BT15 14 N11  
Seaview Ter, Hol. BT18  
*off Birch Dr* 11 AA6  
Sefton Dr BT4 22 U15  
Sefton Pk BT4 22 U15  
Selby Ct BT12 19 K16  
Selby Wk BT12  
*off Selby Ct* 19 K16  
Selkirk Row BT5  
*off Granton Pk* 23 AA17  
Serpentine Gdns, New.  
BT36 9 M4  
Serpentine Par, New.  
BT36 9 N4  
Serpentine Rd, New.  
BT36 9 M4  
Servia St BT12 19 K16  
Sevastopol St BT13 19 J15  
Severn St BT4 21 S15  
Seymour La BT1  
*off Seymour St* 31 E3  
Seymour Row BT1 31 E3  
Seymour St BT1 31 E3  
Seymour St BT2 31 E3  
Shaftesbury Av BT7 20 N18  
Shaftesbury Sq BT2 30 C6  
Shalom Pk BT8 28 V21  
Shamrock Ct BT6  
*off Mount St S* 21 Q17  
Shamrock Pl BT6 21 Q17  
*off Shamrock St* 21 Q17  
Shamrock St BT6 21 Q17  
Shancoole Pk BT14 8 J7  
Shandarragh Pk BT15 8 K8  
Shandon Ct BT5 28 W20  
Shandon Hts BT5  
*off Lower Braniel Rd* 29 X20  
Shandon Pk BT5 22 W18  
Shaneen Pk BT14 8 J7  
Shangarry Pk BT14 8 K7  
Shankill Par BT13 20 L14  
Shankill Rd BT13 19 J14  
Shankill Ter BT13  
*off North  
Boundary St* 20 L14  
Shanlieve Pk BT14 8 K7  
Shanlieve Rd BT11 24 E20  
Shannon Ct BT14 19 K13  
Shannon St BT14 19 K13  
Shanvis Ct BT13 19 K15  
Sharman Cl BT9 26 M22  
Sharman Dr BT9 26 M22  
Sharman Gdns BT9 26 M22  
Sharman Pk BT9 26 M22  
Sharman Rd BT9 26 M21  
Sharman Way BT9 26 M22  
Shaws Av BT11 24 C21  
Shaws Cl BT11 24 B20  
Shaws Ct BT11 24 C21  
Shaws Pk BT11 24 C21  
Shaws Rd BT11 24 C21  
Shaw St BT4 22 U15  
Shelbourne Rd BT6 27 R19  
Sherbrook Cl BT13 20 L14  
Sherbrook Ter BT13  
*off Denmark St* 20 L14  
Sheridan Ct BT15  
*off Sheridan St* 20 M13  
Sheridan St BT15 20 M13  
Sheriff St BT5  
*off Vulcan St* 21 Q15  
Sheringhurst Ct BT15 9 N7  
Sheringhurst Pk BT15 9 N7  
Sherwood St BT6 21 Q17  
Sheskin Way BT6 27 R21  
Shiels St BT12 19 H17  
Shimna Cl BT6 27 R20  
Shipbuoy St BT15 20 N13  
Shore Cres BT15 9 N6  
Shore Rd BT15 14 N10  
Shore Rd, Hol. BT18 11 Z5  
Short Strand BT5 21 Q15  
Short St BT1 20 P13  

Shrewsbury Dr BT9 25 H23  
Shrewsbury Gdns BT9 25 H23  
Shrewsbury Pk BT9 25 J23  
Sicily Pk BT10 25 F23  
Silver Birch Cts BT13 19 K14  
Silvergrove, The BT6 27 S20  
Silverstream Av BT14 13 G9  
Silverstream Cres BT14 13 G9  
Silverstream Dr BT14 13 G9  
Silverstream Gdns  
BT14 13 G9  
Silverstream Par BT14 13 G9  
Silverstream Pk BT14 13 G9  
Silverstream Rd BT14 13 G9  
Silverstream Ter BT14 13 G9  
Silvio St BT13 19 K13  
Sinclair Rd BT3 15 Q11  
Sinclair St BT5 22 V16  
Sintonville Av BT5 21 T16  
Siulnamona Ct BT11  
*off Aitnamona Cres* 24 D19  
Skegoneill Av BT15 14 L9  
Skegoneill Dr BT15 14 M10  
Skegoneill St BT15 14 N10  
Skipper St BT1 31 E1  
Skipton St BT5 21 S16  
Slemish Way BT11 24 E20  
Sliabh Dubh Glen BT12 18 F16  
Sliabh Dubh La BT12 18 F16  
Sliabh Dubh Path BT12 19 G16  
Sliabh Dubh Vw BT12 18 F16  
Sliabh Dubh Wk BT12 19 G16  
Slieveban Dr BT11 24 D21  
Slievecoole Pk BT14 8 K7  
Slievedarragh Pk BT14 8 J7  
Slievegallion Dr BT11 24 D20  
Slievegoland Pk, New.  
BT36 9 M4  
Slievemoyne Pk BT15 8 L8  
Slievetoye Pk BT14 8 J7  
Sloan Ct BT9 25 J19  
Smithfield Mkt BT1  
*off Smithfield Sq N* 30 C1  
Smithfield Sq N BT1 30 C1  
Snugville St BT13 19 K14  
Solway St BT4 21 R15  
Somerdale Gdns BT14 13 G11  
Somerdale Pk BT14 13 G12  
Somerset St BT7 27 P20  
Somerton Cl BT15 8 L8  
Somerton Ct BT15 14 M9  
Somerton Dr BT15 14 M9  
Somerton Gdns BT15 14 M9  
Somerton Gra BT15 9 M7  
Somerton Ms BT15 14 M9  
Somerton Pk BT15 9 M8  
Somerton Rd BT15 9 M8  
Somme Dr BT6 27 S21  
Sorella St BT12 19 J16  
Soudan St BT12 19 J18  
South Bk BT6 27 R21  
South Cl, Hol. BT18 11 Z8  
South Grn BT11 24 D20  
Southland Dale BT5 28 W20  
South Link BT11 24 E20  
South Par BT7 27 P20  
Southport Ct BT14  
*off Mountview St* 14 K12  
South Sperrin BT5 23 AA17  
Southview Cotts BT7  
*off Stranmillis Embk* 26 N19  
Southview St BT7 26 N19  
Southwell St BT15 20 N13  
Spamount St BT15 14 M12  
Spencer St, Hol. BT18 11 AA6  
Sperrin Dr BT5 23 AA17  
Sperrin Pk BT5 23 AA17  
Spiers Pl BT15 19 K14  
Spinnershill La BT14  
*off Old Mill Rd* 12 E9  
Spinner Sq BT12  
*off Leeson St* 19 J16  
Spires, The, Hol. BT18 11 BB7  
Spires Mall Shop BT1 30 C3  
Springdale Gdns BT13 19 G15  
Springfield Av BT12 19 H16  
Springfield Cl BT13 18 F15  
Springfield Ct BT12 19 H15  

Springfield Cres BT12 19 H15  
Springfield Dr BT12 19 H15  
Springfield Hts BT13 18 E15  
Springfield Meadows  
BT13 19 G15  
Springfield Par BT13 19 G15  
Springfield Pk BT13 18 F15  
Springfield Rd BT12 18 D17  
Springhill Av BT12 18 F16  
Springhill Cl BT12 18 F16  
Springhill Cres BT12 18 F16  
Springhill Dr BT12 18 F16  
Springhill Gdns BT12 18 F16  
Springhill Gro BT12 18 F16  
Springhill Hts BT12 18 F16  
Springhill Ri BT12 18 F16  
Springmadden Ct BT12  
*off Springhill Cres* 18 F16  
Springmartin Rd BT13 18 F15  
Springmeadow BT12 19 J16  
Spring Pl BT6  
*off Spring St* 21 Q16  
Spring St BT6 21 Q17  
Springvale Dr BT14 13 F9  
Springvale Gdns BT14 13 F10  
Springvale Par BT14 13 F9  
Springvale Pk BT14 13 F9  
Springview Wk BT13  
*off Malcolmson St* 19 J16  
Squires Hill Cres BT14 13 F9  
Squires Hill Pk BT14 13 F9  
Squires Hill Rd BT14 13 F9  
Squires Vw BT14 13 F8  
Stables, The BT4 22 X13  
Stanfield Pl BT7 31 F4  
Stanfield Row BT7  
*off Lower Stanfield St* 31 G4  
Stanhope Dr BT13 20 L14  
Stanhope St BT13 20 L14  
Stanley Ct BT12 30 A3  
Stanley La BT15  
*off Little York St* 20 N14  
Stanley Pl BT15  
*off Little York St* 20 N14  
Stanley St BT12 30 A3  
Station Ms (Sydenham)  
BT4 22 V13  
Station Rd BT4 22 U13  
Station St BT3 31 G1  
Station St Flyover BT3 31 G1  
Steam Mill La BT1 20 N14  
Steens Back Row BT5  
*off Abetta Par* 21 T17  
Stephen St BT1 20 N14  
Stewarts Pl, Hol. BT18  
*off Strand Av* 11 AA5  
Stewartstown Av BT11 24 B21  
Stewartstown Gdns  
BT11 24 B21  
Stewartstown Ms BT11  
*off Stewartstown Av* 24 C22  
Stewartstown Pk BT11 24 B21  
Stewartstown Rd BT11 24 B22  
Stewart St BT7 31 G5  
Stirling Av BT6 28 T20  
Stirling Gdns BT6 27 S20  
Stirling Rd BT6 27 S20  
Stockmans Av BT11 25 F21  
Stockmans Ct BT11 25 F21  
Stockmans Cres BT11 25 F21  
Stockmans Dr BT11  
*off Stockmans Av* 25 F20  
Stockmans Gdns BT11  
*off Stockmans Av* 25 F21  
Stockmans La BT9 25 F21  
Stockmans La BT11 25 F21  
Stockmans Pk BT11 25 F21  
Stockmans Way BT9 24 E22  
Stoneycairn Ct BT14  
*off Mountainhill Rd* 12 E9  
Stoney Rd BT4 23 BB15  
Stoney Rd (Dundonald)  
BT16 23 BB15  
Stonyford St BT5 21 S16  
Stormont Castle BT4 23 AA14  
Stormont Ct BT4 23 Z16  
Stormont Ms BT4 23 Z16  
Stormont Pk BT4 23 Y16

|  | | |
|---|---|---|
| Victor Pl BT6 | 21 | Q16 |
| Vidor Ct BT4 | | |
| off Victoria Dr | 22 | U14 |
| Vidor Gdns BT4 | 22 | U14 |
| Village Grn, The BT6 | 27 | S19 |
| Violet St BT12 | 19 | J16 |
| Vionville Cl BT5 | 23 | BB18 |
| Vionville Ct BT5 | | |
| off Vionville Ri | 23 | BB18 |
| Vionville Grn BT5 | | |
| off Vionville Ri | 23 | BB18 |
| Vionville Hts BT5 | | |
| off Vionville Ri | 23 | BB18 |
| Vionville Pk BT5 | | |
| off Vionville Ri | 23 | BB18 |
| Vionville Pl BT5 | 23 | BB18 |
| Vionville Ri BT5 | 23 | BB18 |
| Vionville Vw BT5 | 23 | BB18 |
| Vionville Way BT5 | | |
| off Vionville Ri | 23 | BB18 |
| Virginia St BT7 | | |
| off Elm St | 30 | D6 |
| Virginia Way BT7 | 30 | D6 |
| Vistula St BT13 | 19 | J13 |
| Voltaire Gdns, New. | | |
| BT36 | 9 | N4 |
| Vulcan Ct BT5 | | |
| off Vulcan St | 21 | Q15 |
| Vulcan Gdns BT5 | | |
| off Seaforde St | 21 | Q15 |
| Vulcan Link BT5 | | |
| off Vulcan St | 21 | Q15 |
| Vulcan St BT5 | 21 | Q15 |

**W**

|  | | |
|---|---|---|
| Walbeck St BT15 | | |
| off Dawson St | 20 | M13 |
| Walker Ct BT6 | 21 | R17 |
| Walkers La BT1 | | |
| off Frederick St | 20 | M14 |
| Wallasey Pk BT14 | 13 | H9 |
| Walled Gdn, The BT4 | 22 | X13 |
| Wall St BT13 | 20 | M14 |
| Walmer St BT7 | 26 | N20 |
| Walnut Ct BT7 | 31 | E6 |
| Walnut Ms BT7 | 31 | E6 |
| Walnut St BT7 | 31 | E6 |
| Wandsworth Ct BT4 | 22 | W16 |
| Wandsworth Cres BT4 | 22 | W16 |
| Wandsworth Dr BT4 | 22 | W15 |
| Wandsworth Gdns BT4 | 22 | W15 |
| Wandsworth Par BT4 | 22 | W16 |
| Wandsworth Pl BT4 | | |
| off Campbell Pk Av | 22 | W15 |
| Wandsworth Rd BT4 | 22 | W15 |
| Wansbeck St BT9 | 26 | M21 |
| Ward St BT12 | 19 | K15 |
| Waring St BT1 | 31 | E1 |
| Warren Gro BT5 | 29 | X20 |
| Waterford Gdns BT13 | 19 | J15 |
| Waterford St BT13 | 19 | J16 |
| Waterford Way BT13 | | |
| off Waterford St | 19 | J16 |
| Waterloo Gdns BT15 | 9 | M6 |
| Waterloo Pk BT15 | 8 | L6 |
| Waterloo Pk N BT15 | 8 | L6 |
| Waterloo Pk S BT15 | 8 | L6 |
| Watermouth Cres BT12 | 19 | G15 |
| Waterville St BT13 | 19 | J15 |
| Watkins Rd BT3 | 15 | P12 |
| Watt St BT6 | 21 | Q18 |
| Wauchope Ct BT12 | | |
| off Connaught St | 19 | K17 |
| Waveney Av BT15 | 9 | N7 |
| Waveney Dr BT15 | 9 | N7 |
| Waveney Gro BT15 | 9 | N7 |
| Waveney Hts BT15 | 9 | N7 |
| Waveney Pk BT15 | 9 | N7 |
| Wayland St BT5 | 21 | S17 |
| Wayside Cl BT5 | 28 | W20 |
| Weavers Ct BT12 | 30 | A5 |
| Weavershill Ct BT14 | 12 | E9 |
| Weavershill La BT14 | 13 | F9 |
| Weavershill Ms BT14 | 12 | E9 |
| Weavershill Rd BT14 | 12 | E9 |
| Weavershill Wk BT14 | | |
| off Mountainhill Rd | 13 | F9 |
| Welland St BT4 | 21 | S15 |

|  | | |
|---|---|---|
| Wellesley Av BT9 | 26 | L19 |
| Wellington Ct BT1 | | |
| off Wellington St | 30 | C3 |
| Wellington La BT9 | 26 | L19 |
| Wellington Pk BT9 | 26 | L19 |
| Wellington Pk Av BT9 | 26 | L19 |
| Wellington Pk Ter BT9 | 26 | L19 |
| Wellington Pl BT1 | 30 | C3 |
| Wellington St BT1 | 30 | C3 |
| Well Pl BT6 | 21 | Q17 |
| Wellwood Av BT4 | 21 | T14 |
| Wellwood Cl BT4 | | |
| off Wellwood Av | 21 | T14 |
| Wellwood St BT12 | 30 | B5 |
| Welsh St BT7 | 31 | F4 |
| Wesley Ct BT12 | | |
| off Donegall Rd | 30 | C6 |
| Wesley St BT12 | | |
| off Stroud St | 30 | C6 |
| West Bk Cl BT3 | 15 | S8 |
| West Bk Dr BT3 | 15 | S8 |
| West Bk Link BT3 | 15 | S8 |
| West Bk Rd BT3 | 15 | S8 |
| West Bk Way BT3 | 15 | S8 |
| Westbourne St BT5 | 21 | R15 |
| West Circular Cres | | |
| BT13 | 19 | G14 |
| West Circular Rd BT13 | 19 | G15 |
| Westcott St BT5 | | |
| off Bloomfield Av | 21 | T16 |
| West Grn, Hol. BT18 | 11 | Z7 |
| Westhill Way BT12 | | |
| off Glenalina Cres | 18 | E17 |
| Westland Cotts BT14 | 14 | K9 |
| Westland Dr BT14 | 14 | K10 |
| Westland Gdns BT14 | 14 | K10 |
| Westland Rd BT14 | 13 | J10 |
| Westland Way BT14 | 14 | K10 |
| Westlink BT12 | 20 | L14 |
| Westlink BT13 | 20 | L14 |
| West Link, Hol. BT18 | 11 | Z7 |
| Westminster Av BT4 | 21 | T15 |
| Westminster Av N BT4 | | |
| off Westminster Av | 21 | T15 |
| Westminster St BT7 | 20 | N18 |
| Weston Dr BT9 | 25 | G22 |
| Westrock Ct BT12 | 18 | F16 |
| Westrock Cres BT12 | 19 | G16 |
| Westrock Dr BT12 | 18 | F16 |
| Westrock Gdns BT12 | 18 | F16 |
| Westrock Grn BT12 | 18 | F17 |
| Westrock Gro BT12 | | |
| off Westrock Gdns | 19 | G16 |
| Westrock Ms BT12 | 19 | G16 |
| Westrock Par BT12 | 18 | F17 |
| Westrock Pk BT12 | | |
| off Westrock Gdns | 18 | F16 |
| Westrock Pl BT12 | 19 | G17 |
| Westrock Sq BT12 | 19 | G16 |
| Westrock Way BT12 | 19 | G16 |
| Westview Pas BT12 | | |
| off Glenalina Cres | 18 | E17 |
| Westway Cres BT13 | 18 | E13 |
| Westway Dr BT13 | 18 | F13 |
| Westway Gdns BT13 | 12 | E12 |
| Westway Gro BT13 | 18 | E13 |
| Westway Hill BT13 | 18 | E13 |
| Westway Par BT13 | 18 | F13 |
| Westway Pk BT13 | 18 | F13 |
| Wheatfield Ct BT14 | 13 | G10 |
| Wheatfield Cres BT14 | 13 | G11 |
| Wheatfield Dr BT14 | 13 | G10 |
| Wheatfield Gdns BT14 | 13 | G11 |
| Whincroft Rd BT5 | 28 | W19 |
| Whincroft Way BT5 | 28 | W20 |
| Whitecliff Cres BT12 | 18 | F17 |
| Whitecliff Dr BT12 | | |
| off Whiterock Rd | 18 | F17 |
| Whitecliff Par BT12 | | |
| off Whiterock Rd | 18 | F17 |
| Whiterock Cl BT12 | 18 | F17 |
| Whiterock Cres BT12 | 18 | F17 |
| Whiterock Dr BT12 | 18 | F17 |
| Whiterock Gdns BT12 | 18 | F17 |
| Whiterock Gro BT12 | 18 | E17 |

|  | | |
|---|---|---|
| Whiterock Par BT12 | 18 | F17 |
| Whiterock Rd BT12 | 18 | D15 |
| Whitewell Ct, New. | | |
| BT36 | 9 | N4 |
| Whitewell Cres, New. | | |
| BT36 | 9 | N4 |
| Whitewell Dr, New. | | |
| BT36 | 9 | N4 |
| Whitewell Par, New. | | |
| BT36 | 9 | N4 |
| Whitla St BT15 | 15 | P12 |
| Wigton St BT13 | | |
| off Percy Pl | 20 | L14 |
| Wildflower Way BT12 | 25 | H20 |
| Wilgar Cl BT4 | | |
| off Dundela St | 22 | U15 |
| Wilgar St BT4 | 22 | U15 |
| Willesden Pk BT9 | 26 | M22 |
| William Alexander Pk | | |
| BT10 | 24 | D24 |
| William St BT1 | 20 | M14 |
| William St S BT1 | 31 | E2 |
| Willowbank Cres BT6 | 27 | S22 |
| Willowbank Dr BT6 | 27 | R22 |
| Willowbank Gdns BT15 | 14 | L10 |
| Willowbank Pk BT6 | 27 | R22 |
| Willowfield Av BT6 | | |
| off Willowfield Par | 21 | R17 |
| Willowfield Cres BT6 | 21 | R17 |
| Willowfield Dr BT6 | 21 | R17 |
| Willowfield Gdns BT6 | 21 | R17 |
| Willowfield Par BT6 | 21 | R17 |
| Willowfield St BT6 | 21 | R17 |
| Willowfield Wk BT6 | 21 | R17 |
| Willowholme Cres BT6 | | |
| off Willowholme Par | 21 | R18 |
| Willowholme Dr BT6 | 21 | R18 |
| Willowholme Par BT6 | 21 | R18 |
| Willowholme St BT6 | 21 | R18 |
| Willows, The BT6 | 27 | S22 |
| Willow St BT12 | 30 | A3 |
| Willowvale Av BT11 | 24 | C22 |
| Willowvale Gdns BT11 | 24 | C22 |
| Willowvale Ms BT11 | | |
| off Willowvale Gdns | 24 | C22 |
| Wilshere Dr BT4 | 22 | W13 |
| Wilsons Ct BT1 | | |
| off Ann St | 31 | E2 |
| Wilson St BT13 | 30 | B1 |
| Wilton Ct Ms BT13 | | |
| off Canmore St | 19 | J14 |
| Wilton Gdns BT13 | 19 | J14 |
| Wilton St BT13 | 19 | J15 |
| Winchester Ct BT13 | | |
| off Ambleside St | 19 | J13 |
| Windermere Gdns | | |
| BT15 | 8 | K8 |
| Windsor Av BT9 | 26 | K19 |
| Windsor Av, Hol. BT18 | 11 | AA6 |
| Windsor Av N BT9 | 26 | L20 |
| Windsor Cl BT9 | 26 | K20 |
| Windsor Ct BT9 | | |
| off Windsor Pk | 26 | K20 |
| Windsor Dr BT9 | 25 | J19 |
| Windsor Manor BT9 | 26 | K19 |
| Windsor Ms BT9 | 26 | K20 |
| Windsor Pk BT9 | 26 | K20 |
| Windsor Rd BT9 | 25 | J19 |
| Winecellar Entry BT1 | | |
| off Rosemary St | 30 | D1 |
| Winetavern St BT1 | 30 | C1 |
| Wingrove Gdns BT5 | 21 | T17 |
| Winston Gdns BT5 | 22 | W16 |
| Witham St BT4 | 21 | S15 |
| Wolfend Dr BT14 | 13 | F9 |
| Wolfend Way BT14 | | |
| off Hazelbrook Dr | 13 | F8 |
| Wolff Cl BT4 | 21 | Q15 |
| Wolff Rd BT3 | 15 | S11 |
| Wolfhill Av BT14 | | |
| off Ligoniel Pl | 12 | E9 |
| Wolfhill Av S BT14 | 12 | D9 |
| Wolfhill Dr BT14 | 12 | D9 |
| Wolfhill Gdns BT14 | 12 | D8 |
| Wolfhill Gro BT14 | 12 | D8 |
| Wolfhill Manor BT14 | 12 | D8 |
| Wolfhill Rd BT13 | 12 | D10 |
| Wolfhill Rd BT14 | 12 | C8 |

|  | | |
|---|---|---|
| Wolfhill Vw BT14 | | |
| off Mill Av | 12 | E8 |
| Wolseley St BT7 | 20 | M18 |
| Woodbine Ct BT11 | 24 | B22 |
| Woodbourne Cres BT11 | 24 | B22 |
| Woodburn Dr BT15 | 8 | K8 |
| Woodburn St BT13 | | |
| off Downing St | 19 | K14 |
| Woodcot Av BT5 | 21 | T17 |
| Woodcroft Hts BT5 | 28 | W20 |
| Woodcroft Ri BT5 | 28 | W20 |
| Wood End, Hol. BT18 | 11 | Z8 |
| Woodland Av BT14 | 14 | L11 |
| Woodland Gra BT11 | 24 | D23 |
| Woodlands, Hol. BT18 | 11 | BB6 |
| Woodlands Ct BT4 | 22 | X15 |
| Woodlee Ct BT5 | 21 | S17 |
| Woodstock Link BT6 | 21 | Q16 |
| Woodstock Pl BT6 | 21 | Q16 |
| Woodstock Rd BT6 | 21 | Q16 |
| Woodvale Av BT13 | 13 | H14 |
| Woodvale Dr BT13 | 13 | H12 |
| Woodvale Gdns BT13 | 13 | H12 |
| Woodvale Par BT13 | 13 | H13 |
| Woodvale Pass BT13 | 19 | H14 |
| Woodvale Rd BT13 | 13 | H12 |
| Woodvale St BT13 | 19 | H13 |
| Woodview Dr BT5 | 29 | Y19 |
| Woodview Pl BT5 | 29 | Y19 |
| Woodview Ter BT5 | | |
| off Woodview Dr | 29 | Y19 |
| Workman Av BT13 | 19 | H14 |
| Workman Rd BT3 | 15 | S11 |
| Wye St BT4 | | |
| off Dee St | 21 | S15 |
| Wynard Pk BT5 | 21 | X18 |
| Wynchurch Av BT6 | 27 | R22 |
| Wynchurch Cl BT6 | | |
| off Wynchurch Rd | 27 | R22 |
| Wynchurch Gdns BT6 | 27 | R22 |
| Wynchurch Pk BT6 | 27 | R21 |
| Wynchurch Rd BT6 | 27 | R21 |
| Wynchurch Ter BT6 | 27 | Q22 |
| Wynchurch Wk BT6 | 27 | R22 |
| Wyndham Dr BT14 | 14 | K11 |
| Wyndham St BT14 | 14 | K11 |
| Wynfield Ct BT5 | 22 | U16 |
| Wynford St BT5 | | |
| off Moorgate St | 21 | T16 |

**Y**

|  | | |
|---|---|---|
| Yarrow Ct BT14 | | |
| off Yarrow St | 19 | K13 |
| Yarrow St BT14 | 19 | K13 |
| Yew St BT13 | 19 | H13 |
| York Cres BT15 | 14 | N9 |
| York Dr BT15 | 14 | N9 |
| Yorkgate Shop Cen | | |
| BT15 | 20 | N13 |
| York La BT1 | 20 | M14 |
| York Link BT15 | 19 | J13 |
| York Par BT15 | 14 | N9 |
| York Pk BT15 | 14 | N9 |
| York Rd BT15 | 14 | N10 |
| York St BT15 | 20 | M14 |
| Yukon St BT4 | 21 | S15 |

# Tourist and travel information

## Tourist information

Belfast Welcome Centre,
9 Donegall Square North,
Belfast BT1 5GJ
visitbelfast.com

**028 9024 6609**
*048 9024 6609*

Belfast International Airport

**028 9448 4848**
*048 9448 484ξ*

George Best Belfast City Airport

**028 9093 909**
*048 9093 90ς*

## Airport information

Belfast International Airport,
Aldergrove
Belfast BT29 4AB
www.belfastairport.com

**028 9448 484**
*048 9448 484*

George Best Belfast City Airport,
Sydenham Bypass,
Belfast BT3 9JH
www.belfastcityairport.com

**028 9093 9093**
*048 9093 9093*

Map reference 16 U11

## Ferry information

ISLE OF MAN STEAM PACKET CO.
www.steam-packet.com
Belfast to Douglas (April-September)

**08722 992 992**
*00 44 8722 992 992*

STENA LINE www.stenaline.co.uk
Belfast to Cairnryan
Belfast to Birkenhead

**08447 707070**

**Note:** If phoning from GB and Northern Ireland use bold telephone number, if phoning from Republic of Ireland use italic telephone number.